PIPPA MIDDLEHURST
SIMPLE NOODLES

Everyday Recipes,
from Instant
to Udon

Photography by India Hobson
Illustrations by Han Valentine

Hardie Grant

QUADRILLE

For Wren

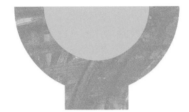

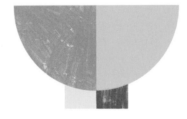

Introduction

For those of you who have been cooking with me since the beginning, you'll know that I love dumplings and noodles, bowls and broths – aka the ingredients, techniques and flavours of East and Southeast Asia. Life has changed a lot for me since writing my first two cookbooks, though. I've had two children, am living with chronic illness and various other challenges that have rendered me pretty squashed for time and, more importantly, energy. And while finding a spare hour to knead, fold and stretch a handmade dough, or watch water, aromatics and seasonings slowly transform into a bowl of flavour will always be a priority for the right occasion, it's rare now that I get to do it for my everyday dinners. And that's life. We adapt.

Now, it's efficiency, nutritiousness, convenience, and speed that dictate what I'm cooking. I utilize my freezer more than ever. I've discovered the joy and ease of the air fryer. One-pot meals rule the roost. Minimal fuss, minimal effort, minimal washing up might be the order of the day, but I will not compromise on maximum flavour.

The meals in this book are mostly inspired by the incredible flavours of East and Southeast Asia, but have gradually changed over time as they became a mainstay in my home kitchen. I skip steps while rushing to get dinner on the table, leave out ingredients that I don't have in the cupboards at the time or sub in leftovers from the fridge. These adaptations occur naturally as part of everyday life. And sometimes they stick.

The traditional, original dishes stand on their own and, of course, require absolutely no tweaking. I wholeheartedly encourage you to try them for a delicious and different experience – I still prepare those versions a lot of the time, when I have the time and the energy. My recipes can be considered as simplified (or devolved) versions designed to be whipped up in no time at all.

I'm grateful to have been able to learn the skills that I have now from many East and Southeast Asian cooks, bloggers and recipe writers, whose names you'll find scattered through this book as inspirations behind flavour pairings, or recommendations for a more in-depth or traditional version of some recipes. You can also find a list of further reading at the back of this book.

Some recipe names have been kept true to their original inspiration, where, although adapted, the dish is not so far removed from the original and remains the same in essence – Weeknight Pad Thai (page 102), for example. Some recipe names have been changed, where enough elements are tweaked, or techniques simplified, to distinguish the dish from its predecessor, with the original dish and inspiration laid out in the recipe intro, such as the Black Bean Mushroom Noodles (page 111). Some dishes are completely made up and their names will reflect this.

These are recipes that are resourceful and realistic. And while ready-made and freezer foods, and instant noodles (all of which you'll find aplenty in these pages) all seem to get an unfair rep – they shouldn't. The assumption is that they're rammed with 'nasty chemicals', 'unhealthy e-numbers' and 'junk additives' or loaded with sugar, salt and fat. But that's simply not the case. It's a common misconception that e-numbers equate to junk, but almost all pre-packaged and shelf-stable foods contain ingredients that are classified by an e-number. That could be E300, also known as vitamin C, or E164 aka saffron, or E160a for beta carotene, which are all naturally occurring. None of them would be perceived as junk if written and presented as the ingredient they are, rather than an e-number.

The stigma surrounding these foods is outdated. It is true that not all convenience foods are made equal, some are full of not-so-nutritious things, but with a little know-how and preparation, a simple packet of instant noodles can become a well-balanced, delicious meal, fit for a solo meal or a dinner to feed family and friends. And your wallet and schedule will thank you for it.

And, of course, there's another kind of fast food you can lean on, too, to elevate your midweek meals. In some recipes in this book, where it's appropriate and will make a dish better, I will suggest ordering certain components from a specified takeaway or restaurant. Think Chinese crispy duck that you can order as an added extra to your Saturday night takeaway, to then use for a speedy noodle dish on a Monday. The combination of home-cooked and chef-prepared is one of my favourite formulas for a fulfilling meal.

As part of my journey, I've also a new-found joy for convenience cookery appliances. I'm precious about my counter-top space and I don't like clutter. However, I finally caved and got an air fryer. I held off for a good while, because you can't hide these things. They're tall, as far as appliances go, and have a large footprint. Well. Let me tell you, it's a revelation. I use it every single day. I'm constantly finding new ways to use it. I can pop stuff into it straight from the freezer or the fridge. I can reheat leftovers. It cooks food perfectly, it's easy to clean, energy efficient and I can turn it on, set the timer and simply walk away. You'll find lots of recipes in the book where air frying would make things even speedier, but don't be put off if you don't have one – I've included oven cooking times, where applicable.

So here is my collection of quick, easy, tasty, feel-good recipes. It's what I'm cooking and eating right now, what I eat when I'm alone, what I crave after a long day. Noodles with love and respect, with sheer ease.

Getting Started

About this book

The chapters in this book are organized with ease of cooking in mind. In recent times, cooking with minimal energy has forced me to consider things I might have previously overlooked when stating how long a recipe might take to prepare. Many variables mean that things won't and don't take the same amount of time for everybody, so I've given ranges for timings for the overall chapters, from 10+ minutes, to 20+ and 30+.

As you move through the chapters, the time and labour involved increases slightly, varying from...

- **really easy noodles**, which includes recipes that can be thrown into one pan, utilize freezer finds and create minimal washing up
- **fuss-free noodles**, which may require a little more chopping or preparation
- **minimal effort noodles**, which includes slightly more involved recipes that might need some quick marinating or roasting in the oven.

The focus, however, remains on simplicity and ease.

Serving sizes

These are varied throughout, but usually serve 2–4 people. All recipes are easily scalable; simply multiply the ingredients as appropriate.

Ingredients

CHILLIES

Deseeding chillies will reduce the overall spice level, while retaining the fruity flavour. You can deseed a chilli by slicing it in half and scraping the seeds out with a spoon.

EGGS

Unless otherwise stated, eggs are medium.

SALT

Unless otherwise stated, sea salt is used throughout.

Sterilizing jars and bottles

Run jars and any lids through a hot cycle in the dishwasher or wash in hot, soapy water, then rinse and drain before putting in the oven (preheated to 120°C/250°F/Gas ½) to dry out for 15 minutes. Carefully remove from the oven and fill while still hot.

Use your freezer

Make the most of your freezer by stocking up on useful ingredients; see page 22 for a list of favourites that are handy to have at home.

DEFROSTING FROZEN SEAFOOD

The recipes in this book often call for frozen seafood. It's important to defrost this fully and safely – ideally in the fridge and inside a container. Check the packaging, as timings can vary depending on size, and allow enough time.

If you cannot defrost food in the fridge, you could put it in a container and then place it under cold running water. Cold water will help to speed up defrosting without allowing the outside of the food to get too warm.

To safely defrost foods in cold water, place in a sealed bag, an airtight container or its original packaging. Fill a clean bowl with cold water and completely submerge the bag/container. Change the water every 30 minutes to ensure it remains cold. Never use warm or hot water, as this can encourage harmful bacteria to grow. Leave the food under running cold water until it has fully defrosted as an alternative to the submerged method. Never defrost raw poultry and meat directly under cold running water, as this can result in harmful bacteria splashed around the kitchen and contamination on surfaces. Always put foods in a sealed container first. Always clean and disinfect the sink before and after defrosting food.

Key

V · VEGETARIAN

VG · VEGAN

Types of Noodles

There is a huge variety of fresh, frozen and dried noodles available for purchase these days, from high-street supermarkets to East and Southeast Asian supermarkets and online. The amount of choice can be confusing and overwhelming, though. Some noodles work really well in most noodle dishes, some only suit specific recipes. Some can be swapped out for others, while some stand on their own. Here, I've suggested swaps for when you don't have a certain type in your cupboard.

In my previous books, we've looked at the science, techniques and recipes for handmade, homemade noodles. But here, we're going to have a look at quick-to-cook and easy-to-keep, noodles. I've suggested some swaps for when you don't have a certain type in your cupboard. In some cases, especially the more unique noodles, there are no good substitutes.

Egg Noodles

There are many, many kinds of noodles that fit under the egg noodles umbrella, and can be used when a recipe calls for such, but they aren't all made equal. Some are thick, some thin, some round, some flat, and some of them have never been within an inch of an egg. At your bigger, everyday supermarkets, you'll likely find packets of 'dried egg noodles' and these are usually fine, albeit non-specific. They might be thick, thin, round or flat and still labelled the same. I don't tend to buy these noodles. If I came across an egg noodle recipe, and I didn't have the specific noodle needed, or the type of noodle wasn't clearly specified, I would use lo mein, long life, wonton, yakisoba, or even spaghetti.

LO MEIN NOODLES

These Chinese noodles can be found fresh, dried, frozen or in steamed-and-ready-to-cook packets. They're probably the most recognizable and versatile of the egg noodles. They are yellow in colour and can be found thinner or slightly thicker. They're what you'd get if you ordered Chow Mein or a stir-fried egg noodle dish from a Chinese takeaway.

Switch for: medium egg noodles

LONG LIFE NOODLES

Also known as yi mein or e-fu noodles, these are (unsurprisingly) a long, egg noodle traditionally served at Chinese banquets to celebrate birthdays, weddings and the Lunar New Year, and are said to bring long life. They're light yellow in colour, round and quite thick. When cooked properly, they're chewy and slightly spongy. They're typically sold dried (the same as instant noodles) and presented in large round nests. Yi mein noodles are usually more expensive than other kinds of egg noodles due to the quality of ingredients and the time they take to make, and the fact that they're used to celebrate special occasions.

Switch for: thick egg noodles

WONTON NOODLES

Said to have originated in Cantonese cuisine, wonton noodles are sold fresh. They are long, very thin, chewy and served in hot broth with wontons, for wonton noodle soup.

Switch for: fine egg noodles, angel hair or capellini pasta

Wheat Noodles

SOMEN NOODLES

A straight, thin, white, Japanese noodle made from wheat flour. They're usually served cold with a dipping sauce, stir fried or in hot broth. Hiyamugi are similar in texture and composition to somen, but are the-next-size-up, if you will, and slightly thicker. They're both delicate in flavour and appearance and typically sold dried, bunched into little portions with a thin slip of paper to bind them.

Switch for: fine wheat noodles or a block of instant noodles

RAMEN NOODLES

Ramen are usually round and crinkly and sold dried, although you can get them fresh, too. These Japanese noodles are made from wheat flour and alkali, which gives the noodle a distinct toothsome texture and chew – this is important, as most ramen noodles are destined to be sat in hot liquid. The alkali changes the bonding properties of the gluten structure within the noodle, which helps prevent a soggy noodle. I use dried ramen noodles at home.

TAIWANESE (KNIFE-PAIRED) NOODLES

Also known, charmingly, as flower petal noodles, Taiwanese noodles are a long, wide wheat noodle with a beautiful frilly edge. This distinct texture comes from the noodles being cut with a knife, rather than a machine. The frilly edge clings to sauces and oils, making them a perfect vessel for thicker sauces with more gubbins. These are one of my favourite noodles, as I love how the frilly edge clings to sauces and dressings so well. They have an amazing chewy and toothsome texture. The brand I use the most is Maioli.

UDON NOODLES

Udon is a Japanese, thick, white wheat noodle. They're chewy, hearty and stand up well to bold flavours or in broth. My favourite way is in a simple but bold dashi stock. You can usually find these frozen, partially cooked in packets, or fresh (page 165).

Switch for: thick wheat noodles

Rice Noodles

HO FUN (OR HO FAN) NOODLES

The critical element to Cantonese Beef Ho Fun (page 69), these are wide, flat rice noodles that are usually sold fresh and can be found in the fridge section of East and Southeast Asian supermarkets. They are chewy in texture and absorb flavour well and are particularly popular in Southern China, especially Guangzhou, where they originate from. In general, rice noodles are more common in the south of China where rice is more abundantly grown, in contrast to wheat/wheat noodles which are more often seen in the north. They need a quick plunge into hot water to loosen them before going straight into a hot wok – what could be easier?

<u>Switch for</u>: wide rice noodles or wide pho noodles

RICE VERMICELLI NOODLES

Also known as rice stick noodles, these are thin, round rice noodles that are dried and sometimes sold in nests. To cook them, they can either be boiled or, more commonly, soaked. Kong Moon is a good brand to look out for.

THAI RICE STICK NOODLES

You can find rice stick noodles in varying widths. I usually have the 5mm (¼in) ones in my cupboard at home and use these for Pad Thai. They come dried and require soaking until al dente, before cooking. Soaking the noodles prevents them from becoming claggy when in contact with the hot wok.

PHO NOODLES

Labelled as banh pho, these Vietnamese rice noodles are flat and wide. They're cooked by soaking or simmering, before being thrown into a steaming bowl of broth. They are slippery and beautifully chewy. My favourite brand is Bamboo Tree.

<u>Switch for</u>: Thai rice stick noodles

Other Noodles

MUNG BEAN NOODLES

A classic in Vietnamese cuisine, often used in fresh spring rolls, mung bean noodles (or cellophane noodles) are not to be confused with rice vermicelli. Their texture, flavour and appearance are much different once cooked, although when dry they could be mistaken for one another. Mung bean noodles are made from mung bean starch, as opposed to wheat or rice flour. Longkou is a brand I use often – the noodles are neatly portioned into little bunches.

SWEET POTATO NOODLES

Another noodle made from starch rather than wheat flour, these utilize sweet potato starch (as the name suggests). Known as dangmyeon in Korean, they're commonly used in the popular Korean dish Japchae (page 155), among others. The texture is slippery and chewy, with a nice bite.

SOBA NOODLES

This Japanese buckwheat noodle, when made traditionally, has only a very small amount of wheat flour, or no wheat flour at all, meaning they have very little or no gluten. This makes the dough fragile and hard to handle. For this reason, you buy the noodles dried. You can find varying ratios of wheat flour/buckwheat flour – typically, the more wheat flour, the cheaper they'll be. Soba's nutty flavour makes them best suited to purposefully simple recipes, which complement but don't overshadow the flavour of the noodle, and in my opinion, they're hard to substitute. My favourite brand of soba is Akagi.

YAKISOBA NOODLES

Also known as mushi chukamen (which translates as steamed Chinese noodles), these are a yellow, thick and round Japanese wheat noodle. They're similar to ramen noodles in texture – chewy and toothsome – when cooked properly. They do not, despite their appearance, contain any egg. Instead, they get their yellow colour from kansui, which brings out the natural yellow pigment in wheat flour, and sometimes food colouring. You will typically find yakisoba noodles packaged pre-cooked, so they can be added straight to the pan from the packet. Dishes that include these noodles are usually called XX Yakisoba, e.g. Vegetable Yakisoba.

Switch for: medium egg noodles or lo mein noodles

SPAGHETTI

Now, stay with me. I appreciate this is contentious, but spaghetti (aka Italian pasta) is often overlooked as a noodle, possibly because it doesn't originate from the same continent as most noodle dishes. Outside of the USA, where spaghetti is referred to as a 'noodle', you would never see it listed as a 'noodle recipe'. I certainly never considered it to be one. Spaghetti is just, spaghetti! But, the definition of noodle is 'a food in the form of long, thin strips made from flour or rice, water, and often egg, cooked in boiling liquid'. Spaghetti is all of those things. It originates in Italy, is round and yellowish and typically made from durum wheat. It is usually sold dry and doesn't contain eggs. I really like the bronze-cut spaghetti, as it leaves a rough and porous texture on the pasta, which is perfect for clinging onto delicious sauces.

Switch for: linguine or medium egg noodles

Equipment

As you might imagine, there's little you'll need by way of specialist equipment in this book, but there are a few things that will certainly make your life easier.

AIR FRYER

Energy and time efficient, this beauty can bake and roast in half the time of an oven, with little excess fat, producing a moreishly crispy result. Definitely worth the counter-top space. Consider me a convert.

FINE GRATER

Having a fine grater, such as a Microplane, will make speedy work of garlic and ginger, which are mainstays in many of these recipes.

FOOD PREP GLOVES

Helpful for tossing dressings through noodles and avoiding chilli or spices permeating the skin.

LARGE, DEEP (RAMEN) BOWLS

While you don't need a specific bowl in which to eat your super quick dinners, having a large, deep bowl to adequately hold slippery noodles and hot broth is a good idea.

MEASURING SPOONS

A good set of measuring spoons will serve you well, whether that be for spices or sauces that are going to lift you out of your recipe rut. They are more accurate than everyday dessertspoons or teaspoons, which can vary wildly between homes, and so are essential for balancing the sweet, sour, salty and spice.

NON-STICK, HEAVY-BASED FRYING PAN (SKILLET) OR WOK

Nearly every recipe in this book will call for a non-stick frying pan (skillet) or wok – and that's because we're cooking fast. Find a pan that is easy to clean and distributes the heat quickly and evenly.

Preparation and Techniques

The methods used in this cookbook are relatively similar throughout and rest upon a couple of tips and techniques that, once you get the hang of them, will enable you to improvise to your heart's content.

PREP, PREP, PREP

The main thing that will set you up for success when cooking on limited time is preparation – have all of your ingredients ready before you set the pan on the heat. Have your garlic grated, your veg peeled and chopped, your protein sliced – whatever it is. Have a pan of boiling water at the ready, for eggs, noodles or veg. When I know dinner time is approaching, I'll fill a pan of water, put it on the hob and let it come to the boil while I do my prepping. Mix your sauce in a jug and set this aside, ready to pour in the pan when it's time. All of these things can be done, and left, until you're ready to cook.

GET IN FORMATION

Knowing the order in which to add the ingredients to the pan is massively helpful, too. Nine times out of ten, I get the best results from using the following sequence: oil, aromatics, protein, fibrous veg that will require a little more cooking, followed shortly after by veg that we want to remain crisp, then noodles, then sauce. Remove the pan from the heat and add any fresh flavours, such as spring onions (scallions) or herbs.

HOW TO PREVENT YOUR NOODLES FROM CLUMPING/STICKING

In most instances, cooking and rinsing noodles can also be done ahead of time. Rinsing the noodles is so important. I often get asked, 'How do I cook a noodle dish without the noodles clumping together?' Noodles stick together because of excess starch that coats them – when heated, starch molecules expand and swell, causing them to burst and release glucose. This causes the starch to interact with water more, causing gelatinization. This occurs on the surface of the noodles when they're cooked, and causes them to become gluey and stick together. We can counteract this by rinsing them thoroughly with cool water, which removes this gluey component from the noodles – this helps them to remain springy, especially when they're going to be reintroduced to heat when stir frying in a wok or pan, for example.

A note on wok hei

Wok hei means 'breath of a wok' – a term coined by Grace Young, in her cookbook of the same name, to describe the inimitable smoky char that wok-fried food will obtain when cooked traditionally over a wok burner.

A traditional wok burner will raise the temperature of the wok to over 400°C (752°F). In traditional wok cookery, a very thin carbon steel wok is used; this heats up quickly and remains hot while over the burner. The food within the wok is tossed, which causes it to hit the sides. These will be dry compared to the base, which will likely contain oil, sauces, juices, etc. that will simply boil rapidly at such high temperatures. The food hitting this dry heat at the sides of the wok causes the smoky, blackened char and unique flavour, known as wok hei.

Shopping List

As we've already begun to touch on, the key to unlocking the true speed and convenience of all of these recipes is prior planning and preparation and that also means stocking up on some kitchen powerhouses – for the cupboard, fridge and freezer – that will work tirelessly, time and again, on your behalf. Here are my favourites, along with some notes to bear in mind before you get started.

Store cupboard essentials

- Chicken bouillon powder – look out for brands like Totole or Knorr
- Chinese dark soy sauce
- Chinese light soy sauce
- Chinese sesame paste
- Chinkiang black rice vinegar
- Cornflour (cornstarch)
- Crispy fried garlic
- Crispy fried shallots
- Doubanjiang
- Dried black fungus mushrooms
- Dried red Chinese chillies
- Dried shiitake mushrooms
- Furikake
- Garlic salt – I like Cornish Sea Salt's Roasted Garlic Salt
- Gochugaru – Korean chilli powder/flakes
- Gochujang – Korean red chilli paste
- Golden caster (superfine) sugar – any white sugar will do for the recipes that call for this, but this is what I have in my pantry
- Hoisin sauce
- Japanese curry blocks – Golden Mountain and Java Curry are great brands
- Japanese soy sauce
- Kimchi – I buy Chongga
- Light (soft) brown sugar
- Maple syrup
- Mirin
- Miso (white)
- Mushroom bouillon powder – again, look out for Totole; all these bouillons contain MSG, which enhances the moreish umami hit from this noodle sauce
- Mushroom stir fry sauce
- Neutral oil – such as rapeseed oil, groundnut oil, vegetable oil and sunflower oil among others
- KMC salt and pepper seasoning
- Sambal oelek
- Shallot sauce – I buy Bull Head
- Shaoxing rice wine
- Sichuan chilli oil or Lao Gan Ma Crispy Chilli Oil
- Sichuan ground chilli (red pepper) flakes
- Sichuan peppercorns (I recommend Da Hong Pao Peppercorns)
- Soy bean sauce
- Sriracha

- Thai oyster sauce
- Thai seasoning sauce
- Thai thin soy sauce
- Thai black soy sauce
- Toasted nori sheet
- Toasted sesame oil
- Ya cai – Sichuan pickled mustard greens
- XO sauce – look out for Two Hot Asians

Fridge essentials

- Bone broth
- Eggs – medium
- Garlic
- Ginger – never throw away your ginger juice!
- Onions
- Pak choi (bok choy)
- Spring onions (scallions)
- TofuKing Spicy Tofu

Frozen essentials

- Dim sum – my favourite brand is Royal Gourmet, the frozen food arm of restaurant business Royal China, the leading Chinese restaurant group in the UK
- Frozen beef tendon balls or beef balls
- Frozen dumplings – my favourite brand is Freshasia.
- Frozen fish balls
- Frozen king prawns – I buy mine already deveined and shelled and I defrost under cold running water
- Frozen squid rings
- Frozen wontons – Royal Gourmet also sell amazing wontons, which are perfect on their own or for making a super-quick version of Cantonese wonton noodle soup

Instant Noodles

You can easily jazz up instant noodles, depending on what you're in the mood for; however, this does rely on having – at the very least – a couple of toppings in the fridge or freezer, some instant noodles on-hand and a little know-how.

A well-stocked selection of noodles, an equally well-stocked fridge and freezer and knowing just what tastes good with what, on the other hand, will widen your options exponentially – giving you unlimited options when your noodle craving hits.

So, here are some ways that I serve my favourite instant noodles. As is the nature of instant noodles, you can cobble most of these together in less than 15 minutes. Substitutions are welcomed and encouraged – tailor to your taste!

Mix and match the opposite to make your equations. The suggestions on the following pages each serve one. With most of these bowls, I would use just one pot of boiling water to cook each element. You can do this at the same time, or one by one. Then I assemble the seasoning sachets, as directed, in the bowl. If the instant noodles are the soupy kind, I use fresh water from the kettle to make up the broth with the seasonings and not the noodle/ingredient cooking water.

STORE CUPBOARD

Crispy fried garlic

Crispy fried shallots

Pickled gherkins

Sichuan chilli oil or Lao Gan Ma Crispy Chilli Oil

Spam

Toasted nori sheets

Ya cai

FRIDGE

Bean sprouts

Crab sticks/seafood sticks

Coriander (cilantro)

Cucumber

Cut kimchi

Eggs

Greens such as choi sum, courgette (zucchini), long-stemmed broccoli and pak choi (bok choy)

Mushrooms – shimeji and enoki are my favourite

Rotisserie chicken

Spring onions (scallions)

Tofu puffs

FREEZER

Beef balls

Chinese fish cake

Fish balls (I like fried prawn/shrimp balls)

Frozen dumplings (I like Freshasia)

Frozen king prawns (jumbo shrimp)

Frozen squid rings

Unagi

INSTANT NOODLES

Baijia Shanxi

Indomie Mi Goreng

Indomie Mi Goreng Rendang

Kiki Noodles Spring Onion (Scallion)

Mom's Dry Noodle Dan Dan

Mom's Dry Noodle Sour and Spicy

Mykuali Penang White Curry

Nongshim Neoguri

Nongshim Shin Ramyun

Prima Taste Chilli Crab

Prima Taste Laksa

Spicy,
Soupy,
Seafoody

Bring a pan of water to the boil and set a timer for 5 minutes. Add the seafood and fish balls (depending on brand, make sure to check the packet instructions for notes on cooking from frozen), cook for 2 minutes. Add the noodles and cook for a further 2 minutes. Add the greens and blanch for 30 seconds. Add the bean sprouts and blanch for 30 seconds. Remove from the heat and scoop out the seafood, fish balls and veg and set aside. Strain the noodles into a colander. Add the noodle seasoning sachets to a deep bowl. Add 350ml (12fl oz) freshly boiled water and mix to combine. Add the noodles to the broth and top with the seafood, fish balls and veg, and garnish with spring onion (scallion).

3 frozen prawns (shrimp)

3 frozen squid rings

3 frozen fish balls

Mykuali Penang White Curry Noodles

1 small handful of greens, choi sum or pak choi (bok choy)

1 small handful of bean sprouts

Mykuali Penang White Curry Seasoning

1 spring onion (scallion), chopped

Umami, Savoury, Moreish

Bring a pan of water to the boil and drop in the noodles, greens and shimeji mushrooms. Cook for 3 minutes. At the same time, fry an egg until cooked the way you like (I like a runny yolk). Add the noodle seasoning to a deep bowl. Scoop the noodles, greens and mushrooms from the pan with a slotted spoon and pop straight into the bowl with the seasoning, then toss well to coat. Top with crispy shallots, spring onion (scallion), shredded chicken and the fried egg.

Indomie Mi Goreng

1 small handful of greens, choi sum or pak choi (bok choy)

1 small handful of shimeji mushrooms

1 egg

noodle seasoning

1 tbsp crispy shallots

1 spring onion (scallion), finely chopped

1 handful of rotisserie chicken/ leftover roasted chicken, shredded

Really Easy Noodles

10+ MINUTES

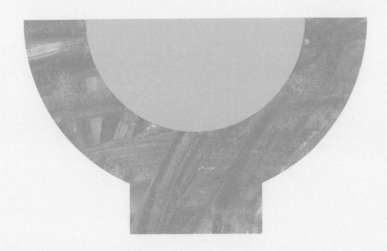

Sichuan-style Sesame Noodles

SERVES 2 · VG

2 tbsp Chinese sesame paste
1 tsp peanut butter
2 tbsp light soy sauce
1 tbsp Sichuan chilli oil or Lao Gan
   Ma Crispy Chilli Oil
1 tbsp Chinkiang black rice vinegar
1 tsp golden caster (superfine)
   sugar
1 tsp toasted sesame oil
½ tsp mushroom bouillon powder
2 nests fresh wheat noodles
1 spring onion (scallion),
   finely diced
¼ cucumber, finely shredded

Sesame noodles are one of those dishes that appear super-simple but take precise tweaking, practice and experience to get exactly right. The quality of the Chinese sesame paste makes a big difference. The best I have ever tried was in a restaurant called Ji Gai He on Ji'an Lu in Shanghai – my friend and former food critic Betty Richardson (@bettyshanghai, on Instagram) took me there and I have longed for them ever since. The noodles were super long and perfectly al dente, the sauce was silky smooth, the flavour was nutty and moreish with a little fresh hit of spring onion (scallion). It was perfection.

Peanut butter wouldn't typically be added to this sauce, but I like the extra nutty hit it gives – leave it out if you prefer. It can be served hot or cold.

1   Combine the sesame paste, peanut butter, light soy sauce, chilli oil, vinegar, sugar, sesame oil, bouillon powder and 4 tbsp boiling water in a large mixing bowl and carefully stir until everything is dissolved. Chinese sesame paste is quite thick and firm, so it can take a while to dissolve until smooth. To help the process along, you can use a blender to make a smooth sauce, just be careful with hot liquids.

2   Cook the noodles according to the packet instructions or until al dente. Strain and rinse under cool water, separating the noodles with your fingers, to prevent them from sticking. If serving cold, rinse under cold water for 3–4 minutes. Add the noodles straight into the mixing bowl containing the sauce and toss to coat. Divide the noodles immediately between bowls and top with any remaining sauce, spring onion (scallion) and cucumber. Add extra chilli oil if desired.

King Prawn XO Butter Noodles

SERVES 2

120g (4¼oz) bronze-cut spaghetti
  or 2 nests egg noodles
2 tbsp salted butter
2 tbsp XO sauce
1 tbsp light soy sauce
½ tbsp dark soy sauce
2 tsp golden caster (superfine)
  sugar
10 king prawns (jumbo shrimp),
  defrosted if frozen
200g (7oz) pak choi (bok choy),
  leaves separated

XO sauce is made up of dried seafood and ham, with aromatics like garlic and chilli, and so is full of super-charged salty, umami flavours. XO is shorthand for luxury in Hong Kong where it originates, which is no surprise as dried seafood is expensive. A good jar of XO sauce might cost upwards of £5, but it's definitely worth it. It can be used as a condiment for rice or, as here, to make a sauce for noodles. My friend and small business owner Ana Da Costa makes a great version – look out for Two Hot Asians. She dehydrates scallops herself and it's one of the best XO sauces I've ever had.

Prawns are commonly combined with XO sauce, but if you don't have them, you could use any protein you choose. The sauce is what makes this dish.

1   Bring a pan of salted water to the boil and drop in your chosen noodles. Cook according to the packet instructions. Once cooked, strain in a colander and rinse under cool water for 1 minute, separating the noodles with your fingers, to prevent them from sticking. Set aside.

2   While the noodles bubble away, heat the butter in a deep, non-stick, heavy-based frying pan (skillet). Add the XO sauce, soy sauces and sugar with about 4 tbsp of noodle cooking water. Bring the sauce to a bubble and stir until the sugar dissolves. Add the prawns (shrimp) and pak choi (bok choy) and cook for 4–5 minutes until the prawns are pink and the greens are wilted. Remove the pan from the heat, add the noodles and toss to coat them in the sauce. Serve immediately.

Kimchi Honey Fried Noodles

SERVES 2 · V

2 nests thick wheat noodles
1 tbsp neutral oil
2 garlic cloves, grated
½ carrot, grated
100g (3½oz) cut kimchi, with juice
1 tbsp gochujang
1 tsp gochugaru
1 tbsp light soy sauce
1½ tbsp runny honey
1 spring onion (scallion),
   finely diced
1 tbsp toasted sesame seeds

Korean kimchi is a super-star ingredient. It has amazing health benefits (because it is fermented it feeds the good bacteria in our guts), is versatile (you can eat it straight from the tub or cook with it), it tastes amazing and it gets better with age. My favourite brand is Chongga, which you can find in the fridge section of East and Southeast Asian supermarkets. I get the cut cabbage kimchi (mat kimchi), but you can also get whole cabbage kimchi (tongbaechu kimchi), where the cabbage leaves come uncut, or you can find other varieties such as yeolmu kimchi, which is made with young summer radish. Any of them would work well here.

During the Joseon dynasty, honey was reserved for the higher classes and was not readily available to all. Honey, therefore, became a prized ingredient in South Korea, synonymous with decadence. It's common to see honey as the sweetener, or as the dominant flavour profile in both sweet and savoury Korean recipes – think, honey butter chicken, Heoni-beoteo-chikin – and the combination of spicy kimchi, or gochujang, and sweet honey is very popular. It's a sweet-spicy flavour contrast I am wild about.

1   Cook the noodles according to the packet instructions or until al dente. Strain and rinse under cool water, separating the noodles with your fingers, to prevent them from sticking. Set aside.

2   Heat the oil in a non-stick, heavy-based frying pan (skillet) over a medium-high heat. Add the garlic and fry for 30 seconds or until fragrant. Add the carrots and stir fry quickly for 1 minute, until just softened. Add the kimchi with its juice and stir fry for another minute, allowing the juice to bubble. Add the gochujang, gochugaru, soy sauce and runny honey and stir to combine.

3   Add the noodles to the pan and toss well so the noodles are coated in the sauce. Serve immediately topped with diced spring onion (scallion) and toasted sesame seeds.

Tomato Egg Noodles

SERVES 2 · V

1 tbsp neutral oil

3 eggs, beaten

2 spring onions (scallions), thickly sliced

2 large garlic cloves, crushed or grated

250g (9oz) very ripe vine tomatoes, diced

¼ tsp sea salt

2 tsp golden caster (superfine) sugar

2 tbsp Shaoxing rice wine

2 nests fresh or dried thick wheat noodles

1 tsp toasted sesame oil

¼ tsp freshly ground black pepper

Tomato egg stir fry is a quick and easy, meat-free dish known as Jia Chang Cai – the epitome of Chinese home cookery and a comforting classic of which every family has their own version. I love food writer and photographer Wei Guo's recipe for egg and tomato stir fry – it's one I've made countless times, and it only uses 3 ingredients. It's usually served with rice, or as part of a whole meal but, you've guessed it, it's also really great with noodles.

It's best to use super ripe, juicy tomatoes when they're in season. We're talking home-grown or local farmers' market, if you can. Same for the eggs – the better quality you buy, the better this dish will taste. With so few ingredients, it makes all the difference.

1   Heat half the neutral oil in a non-stick, heavy-based frying pan (skillet) or wok over a medium-high heat. Add the beaten eggs and scramble lightly, until just cooked. Remove from the pan and set aside.

2   Wipe the pan, add the remaining oil, the spring onions (scallions) and garlic. Stir fry for 30 seconds until fragrant, then add the diced tomatoes. Season with the salt and sugar. Stir fry for another minute, before adding the Shaoxing rice wine. Allow this to bubble for 1 minute before adding 100ml (3½oz) water and cook for 5 minutes, until the tomatoes soften and turn to a sauce-like consistency.

3   Meanwhile, cook the noodles according to the packet instructions. Strain and rinse under cool water, separating the noodles with your fingers, to prevent them from sticking. Dress with the sesame oil and divide between two bowls.

4   Add the scrambled eggs back into the tomato pan, stir to combine, and season with black pepper. Serve over the noodles immediately, while everything is piping hot.

Garlic Butter Miso Noodles

SERVES 2 · V

120g (4¼oz) bronze-cut spaghetti
   or 2 nests lo mein thick egg
   noodles
1 tbsp white miso
2 tsp mirin
1 tsp dark soy sauce
2 tsp light soy sauce
½ tsp golden caster (superfine)
   sugar
2 tbsp butter
4 garlic cloves, finely grated
1 spring onion (scallion),
   finely chopped

I love butter and I love miso. You can probably tell that I prefer salty to sweet, and butter and miso are the pinnacle salt contributors you can have in a meal, in my eyes. Add garlic to this mix and we've reached perfection.

1   Bring a pan of water to the boil and cook your chosen noodles until just al dente, reserving the water.

2   Meanwhile, combine the miso, mirin, dark soy, light soy and sugar in a jug (pitcher). Heat a non-stick, heavy-based frying pan (skillet) over a medium heat and add the butter and garlic. Fry the garlic for 30 seconds or until fragrant, before adding the miso mixture. Add a couple of tablespoons of the noodle water. Stir well until a smooth sauce forms, then reduce the heat.

3   Once the noodles are cooked, transfer from the boiling water straight into the miso sauce with a pair of tongs. Toss well to combine, adding an extra splash of noodle water if the sauce is looking a little thick. Add the spring onion (scallion) and toss through. Serve immediately.

Spicy Tofu Noodles

SERVES 4 · V

4 nests soba noodles
200g (7oz) green beans, trimmed
  and halved
230g (8oz) TofuKing Spicy Tofu
2 tbsp light soy sauce
2 tbsp Chinkiang black rice vinegar
2 spring onions (scallions), sliced
4 fried eggs (optional)

TofuKing Spicy Tofu is a revelation to me. Found in good Chinese supermarkets, vacuum-packed in the fridge section, it's spicy and moreishly tasty. I could eat a whole packet on its own; however, I think it's next level when served with noodles. It is a pressed firm tofu, with a texture very similar to seitan – making it chewy and toothsome, like meat. And the usual suspects in the marinade – chilli oil, garlic, sugar – among other things, make it taste so good. The marinade makes a perfect dressing for noodles, which means this recipe is a minimal fuss, minimal mess, one-pan dish. Although, if you're in the mood, a fried egg on top is really great (omit to make it vegan).

1   Bring a large pan of water to the boil and add the soba noodles and green beans. Cook for 4 minutes on a rolling boil.

2   Meanwhile, pierce a hole in the tofu packet and heat in the microwave for 45 seconds. Or stir fry quickly for 5 minutes, if you don't have a microwave.

3   Once the noodles are cooked, tip into a colander and rinse under cool water, separating the noodles with your fingers, to prevent them from sticking. Add the noodles back to the pan, along with the tofu and its marinade (when you open the packet, hot steam may escape, so do this carefully). Add the soy sauce, vinegar and spring onions (scallions). Toss to coat and serve. Top each portion with a fried egg, if you like.

Shallot Sauce Noodles

SERVES 2

2 tbsp Bull Head Shallot Sauce

2 tsp chicken bouillon powder

2 tbsp light soy sauce

1 tsp dark soy sauce

1 tbsp Chinkiang black rice vinegar

1 tsp Sichuan chilli (red pepper) flakes or gochugaru

¼ tsp freshly ground black pepper

2 nests Taiwanese flower petal noodles

2 spring onions (scallions), finely shredded

1 tbsp crispy shallots

Taiwanese Bull Head Shallot Sauce is a moreish, super savoury condiment – so good that I would (and do) eat it on toast. More traditionally, it can be served over rice or used as a dip. It's a great way to inject umami into a dish in super-quick time – think of onions that have been caramelized in butter for hours and hours until they're reduced, sticky and delicious. It's that, but ready and waiting in your pantry.

This recipe comes together in the time it takes to cook the noodles, but don't be deceived by its simplicity.

1   Add the shallot sauce, chicken bouillon powder, light soy, dark soy, vinegar, chilli (red pepper) flakes and black pepper to a large mixing bowl and stir well to combine.

2   Cook the noodles according to the packet instructions. Scoop from the cooking water, using tongs, straight into the mixing bowl containing the sauce. Toss well to coat and serve garnished with the shredded spring onion (scallion) and crispy shallots.

Tinned Mackerel Soba

SERVES 2

2 nests dried soba noodles
1 handful of frozen peas
1 tbsp light soy sauce
1 tsp toasted sesame oil
1 tsp maple syrup
¼ tsp freshly ground black pepper
1 x 82g (3oz) tin mackerel, in oil
  or brine
2 spring onions (scallions),
  finely sliced
1 tbsp furikake

Tinned mackerel is nostalgic for me. I have memories of early childhood, my dad sat in the bathroom in his underwear, eating tinned mackerel, straight from the tin with a fork. I was sat at his feet and he would present a forkful for me, then take one himself, with a knowing smile. I remember sitting there, sharing this treat with him in silence, and it feeling like I was being allowed to share something special. A secret ritual. His quiet time.

I don't have many memories of my dad living at home, he and my mum split when I was 3, and he must have only been 25 or 26 at that time. And I, not much older than 2. Of course, then, I just saw him as my dad, a man, a grown-up, one of my caregivers, but looking back now, being a mum in my 30s, I think of how young he was. How young they were. And how hard it must have been for them, my parents, in their twenties, raising three children through rough times, trying their best. And I know how rare it is to have solitude and quiet time when you have young children. How rare it is to be granted five minutes alone. Just to eat something in peace.

Looking back on that memory, objectively, and knowing and feeling the context, the young man, trying and failing to steal some seclusion – I think how precious that is, and how precious life is. And how silly it is that a tin of mackerel can evoke such emotion.

Soba noodles served with fish is a classic Japanese combination. Nishin Soba comprises hot soba with herring, and Zaru Soba – cold soba noodles – might often be served with a side of grilled mackerel (Saba No Shioyaki).

1   Bring a pan of water to the boil and drop in the soba noodles and the peas. Cook for the time stated on the noodle packet (this is usually around 4 minutes).

2   Meanwhile, combine the light soy sauce, sesame oil and maple syrup with the black pepper in a jug (pitcher) to make the sauce. Drain the tinned fish of its oil or brine.

3   Once the noodles are cooked, strain them and return the noodles and peas to the pan. Flake in the mackerel using a fork, add the spring onions (scallions) and the sauce. Mix everything well. Serve, topped with furikake.

Midnight Noodles and Dumplings

SERVES 1

4 frozen dumplings (any flavour)
1 nest dried ramen noodles
1 small handful of greens
   (long-stemmed broccoli,
   choi sum, pak choi/bok choy,
   mange tout/snow peas, etc.
   all work well)
1 tbsp light soy sauce
1 tsp kecap manis
1 tsp Sichuan chilli oil or Lao Gan
   Ma Crispy Chilli Oil
1 tsp maple syrup
1 tsp crispy fried garlic

This is one of those recipes that pops into my head if I can't sleep, when I'm hungry and need something low maintenance and quick, which doesn't require any chopping and comes together in one pan. It's the sort of thing where you can nip downstairs and return to bed with a steaming bowl of something good, in the blink of an eye. But, it really is great at any time.

My favourite brand of frozen dumpling is Freshasia – you can find them in the freezers at East and Southeast Asian supermarkets, and they have a huge variety of flavours. My favourites are prawn and sweetcorn or lamb and cumin, depending on my mood.

1 Bring a pan of water to the boil and drop in the frozen dumplings. Cook for 2 minutes, then add the noodles and the greens to the same pot. Cook for the time stated on the noodle packet.

2 Pop everything into a colander and strain, before tipping everything into a large ramen or pasta bowl.

3 Combine the light soy, kecap manis, Sichuan chilli oil and maple syrup in a jug (pitcher). Add the sauce to the noodles and toss to coat. Sprinkle with crispy garlic. Sneak back up to bed and devour in silence.

Movie Night Ramen

SERVES 2

1 egg
2 nests somen or dried or fresh thin
   wheat noodles
500ml (17fl oz) chicken stock or
   bone broth
1 tsp chicken bouillon powder
2 tsp toasted sesame oil
2 tbsp light soy sauce
1 tsp light (soft) brown sugar
160g (5½oz) thick-cut roast ham
2 spring onions (scallions), sliced

Ponyo is a Studio Ghibli animation and one of my favourite comfort movies. It's one of my daughter Peggy's favourites, too. The plot is Hayao Miyazaki's interpretation of the tale of *The Little Mermaid*, with modern themes including environmental degradation. It's beautiful to watch.

In the film, there is a scene when Ponyo, having freshly emerged from her ocean home, befriending a human child and growing legs, is served a bowl of steaming hot ramen, served with ham and boiled eggs. This is the first time Ponyo has ever seen ramen, and the scene perfectly captures a childlike sense of wonder and amusement. Ponyo loves the ham.

The way I prepare this dish at home is much like a simple soy sauce ramen. As with most simple dishes, the ingredients speak for themselves, so use the best possible chicken stock you have or can find. Homemade is preferable, but if using store bought (which I often do), try to find a decent bone broth with plenty of fat.

1   Bring a pan of water to the boil and drop in the egg. Set a timer for 6 minutes 45 seconds. Add the noodles to the same pan for the time stated on the packet. Once cooked, strain the noodles and egg into a colander and rinse under cool water. When cool enough to handle, peel the egg and carefully cut in half.

2   Meanwhile, heat the stock or bone broth gently until steaming hot.

3   Into each serving bowl add ½ tsp chicken bouillon powder, 1 tsp sesame oil, 1 tbsp light soy, ½ tsp sugar and half the stock or bone broth. Mix well to combine.

4   Divide the noodles, ham, egg and spring onions (scallions) between the bowls. Allow the ham to heat up in the hot broth for a couple of minutes before serving.

Golden Noodle Soup

SERVES 2

100g (3½oz) ginger, peeled
100g (3½oz) turmeric, peeled
600ml (21fl oz) vegetable or
   chicken stock
2 tbsp light soy sauce
2 tsp light (soft) brown sugar
1 tbsp toasted sesame oil
1 handful of frozen peas
1 handful of spring greens,
   cabbage, kale or cavolo
   nero, finely sliced
100g (3½oz) shimeji mushrooms
2 nests rice vermicelli noodles
1 small handful of coriander
   (cilantro), roughly chopped
1 small handful of chives,
   roughly chopped
1 small handful of shredded
   leftover roast chicken (optional)

Sometimes, if I'm out and about working, feeling tired and sluggish, I'll get one of those shots of cold-pressed ginger and turmeric juice, and it instantly wakes me up. The spicy zing from the ginger always makes me feel so much better. And it's this that I wanted to recreate in a bowl of noodles.

You will need fresh turmeric for this, but if you can't get hold of it, just leave it out – don't use ground turmeric. And if you want to make this vegan, leave out the chicken and use vegetable stock.

1   Add the ginger and turmeric to a mini blender with 2 tbsp water and whizz to form a paste. Add this to a very fine sieve (strainer) or muslin (cheesecloth) and squeeze the juice into a pan. Add the stock and set over a medium heat to warm through. Season with the light soy sauce, sugar and sesame oil. Combine well and taste – adjust the seasonings as necessary.

2   Meanwhile, bring a pan of water to the boil and add the peas, spring greens and mushrooms. Cook for 1–2 minutes, until the greens are softened but still vibrant green and the mushrooms are just cooked. Cook the noodles in the same pot, according to the packet instructions.

3   Divide the noodles and vegetables between two deep bowls and top with the hot broth. Garnish with herbs and leftover chicken, if using.

One-pot Kimchi Ramen

SERVES 2

2 hotdogs (optional)
1 tbsp neutral oil
2 garlic cloves, grated or crushed
80g (3oz) cut kimchi
1 tbsp gochujang
2 tsp gochugaru
600ml (21fl oz) chicken or
    vegetable stock
1 tbsp light soy sauce
2 tsp maple syrup
1 tsp toasted sesame oil
½ tsp chicken or mushroom
    bouillon powder
2 nests ramen noodles
2 egg yolks
1 spring onion (scallion),
    finely sliced

I'm not sure this recipe needs much introduction, apart from maybe to say – if you haven't tried octodogs yet, I recommend trying octodogs.

Known as 'ramyun' in Korea, instant packet noodles are a common Korean dish in their own right – and now totally distinct from their Japanese instant noodles predecessor. Nongshim Shin Ramyun is perhaps one of the most popular instant noodle brands to come out of South Korea, alongside Samyang Buldak spicy Korean ramyun.

Throwing everything into one pot, as below, is a technique used in the well-known South Korean dish Budae Jjigae, or Army Stew, which rose to popularity in the US military bases after the Korean War. Shelf-stable foods such as processed meats, baked beans and burger cheese slices were cooked together in a single pot, flavoured with gochujang and kimchi, with ramyun noodles thrown in. And, of course, I love it because it saves on washing up!

1   If using hotdogs, slice them in half and create octodogs by making 4 slices from the cut-end of the hotdog, halfway up, to create little legs. Do this on all 4 hotdog halves. Set aside

2   Heat the neutral oil in a heavy-based pan or casserole over a medium-high heat. Add the garlic and stir fry for 30 seconds before adding the kimchi. Stir fry for another 30 seconds. Add the gochujang and gochugaru and mix well. Cook for 1 minute, then add the stock and combine. Season with the light soy sauce, maple syrup, sesame oil and bouillon powder.

3   Bring the stock to a gentle simmer and add the ramen noodles and octodogs, if using. Cover the pan with a lid and cook for 2–3 minutes, until the noodles are beginning to soften. Stir once, to ensure the noodles are completely submerged in the broth. Cook for a further 2 minutes.

4   Divide the tangle of kimchi noodles between two bowls. Top with the octodogs, an egg yolk and sliced spring onions (scallions).

Spicy Korean Cold Noodles

SERVES 2

1 egg
2 nests somen or thin
  wheat noodles
300g (10½oz) cut kimchi,
  with juice
3 tbsp gochujang
2 tbsp maple syrup
1 tbsp light soy sauce
2 tsp toasted sesame oil
2 tsp gochugaru
2 garlic cloves, crushed or grated
½ cucumber, deseeded and
  finely shredded
1 tbsp toasted sesame seeds
1 toasted nori sheet (optional)

Bibim Guksu is a Korean dish of chilled wheat noodles dressed in a spicy sauce, topped with refreshing cucumber and a boiled egg. I make it on hot summer days, when the heat feels inescapable. Many Koreans believe that eating spicy food during hot weather is a great way to cool down, as it promotes sweating – the body's natural cooling system. Fighting fire with fire!

1   Bring a pan of water to the boil. Drop in the egg and set the timer to 7 minutes. Cook the noodles in the same pan, alongside the egg, according to the packet instructions. Strain and rinse with cold water until they are completely cool. Pluck out the egg and, when cool enough to handle, peel and carefully cut in half. Set aside.

2   Combine 200g (7oz) of the cut kimchi and its juice, the gochujang, maple syrup, light soy sauce, sesame oil, gochugaru and garlic in a large mixing bowl and mix well to make the sauce. Tip the noodles in and mix through (using your hands is best for this – wearing food prep gloves is advisable).

3   Divide the noodles between two bowls. Top each with finely shredded cucumber, an egg half, toasted sesame seeds and the remaining kimchi. If using nori, cut into very thin strips using kitchen scissors, and serve on top of the noodles. Serve at room temperature.

Simple Sesame Soba

SERVES 4

4 nests dried soba noodles
1 small carrot, grated
3 spring onions (scallions),
    finely sliced
2 tbsp Chinese sesame paste
    or tahini
2 tbsp light soy sauce
1 tbsp Chinkiang black rice vinegar
1 tbsp maple syrup
1 tbsp toasted sesame oil
½ tsp mushroom bouillon powder
300–400g (14oz) shredded
    leftover roast chicken (optional)
1 tbsp toasted sesame seeds
1 tbsp furikake
2 tbsp Sichuan chilli oil or Lao Gan
    Ma Crispy Chilli Oil (optional)

I'll often make this Japanese-style noodle dressing in bulk (multiply the recipe by 2 or 4) in a sterilized jar and keep in the fridge for up to 2 weeks. The brand of soba noodles I buy, Akagi, cooks in 4 minutes – so when I'm hungry and really short on time, I know I can have a meal in less than 10 minutes. I like to make this dish more substantial with some leftover rotisserie chicken, but you could throw in leftover beef or pork, too, or skip the meat altogether to keep it vegan.

1   Cook the noodles according to the packet instructions. Strain and rinse under cold water until completely cool. Place into a mixing bowl with the carrot and spring onions (scallions) and toss through.

2   In a high-speed blender or jug (pitcher) with a stick blender, combine the sesame paste, light soy sauce, vinegar, maple syrup, sesame oil, mushroom bouillon powder and 5 tbsp boiling water until smooth. Pour into the mixing bowl with the noodles and vegetables. Add the chicken, if using, and toss through using your hands (with food prep gloves) or tongs.

3   Serve at room temperature, divided between four bowls, topped with the toasted sesame seeds and furikake. Drizzle over some chilli oil, if you fancy a kick.

Simple Veggie Yakisoba

SERVES 2

½ onion, sliced
½ large carrot, finely shredded
½ small sweetheart (hispi) cabbage
  or Chinese leaf (napa cabbage),
  sliced
6 fresh shiitake or chestnut
  (cremini) mushrooms, sliced
½ red (bell) pepper, sliced
2 nests fresh yakisoba noodles
2 tbsp neutral oil
2 spring onions (scallions),
  finely shredded

For the sauce
5 tbsp Yakisoba sauce, or:

3 tbsp Japanese Worcestershire
  sauce (I use Bulldog)
1 tbsp light soy sauce
1 tsp dark soy sauce
1 tbsp golden caster (superfine)
  sugar
2 tbsp oyster sauce
¼ tsp sea salt
2 tbsp ketchup
1 tsp toasted sesame oil

To serve (optional)
1 tbsp ground nori powder
2 tsp pickled ginger

Yakisoba roughly translated means stir fried noodles – yaki, meaning 'cooked over direct heat' and soba meaning 'noodles'. Traditionally, they'll be cooked in a Teppanyaki restaurant (a teppan is a large flat grill plate) that also serves okonomiyaki, a thick, grilled Japanese pancake, which is also cooked on a teppan.

I have fond memories of eating this dish on the go in Japan. Japanese convenience stores, known as konbini, are 24/7 one-stop shops, and are equipped with everything you might need for a meal out and about, often with seating in and outside the stores themselves and facilities to heat your food and cool your drinks. From onigiri, to bento, sandwiches, instant noodles and oden, the choice is vast and delicious. You can pick up a yakisoba pan, which is noodles stuffed inside a hot dog bun, from any 7-Eleven. However, the best yakisoba I have tried was in a teppanyaki restaurant called Manmaru No Tsuki in Kyoto.

Before I'd ever stepped foot in Japan I would eat this dish from a conveyor-belt Japanese restaurant in Manchester with my best friend when we were 14. It's a dish I've always loved.

You can use yakisoba sauce to make this recipe even quicker – I love Otafuku yakisoba sauce – but I've also included the recipe for a homemade version if you can't get hold of any.

1   Prepare all the vegetables in advance, and have them ready to go. If you're making the sauce yourself, mix this in a jug (pitcher) and set aside. Put the yakisoba noodles into a sieve (strainer). Set aside.

2   Heat the neutral oil in the biggest non-stick, heavy-based frying pan (skillet) you've got or, even better, a plancha, over a medium-high heat. Add the onion, carrot and cabbage and stir fry for 2–3 minutes. Allow them to sit in the pan without stirring for 1–2 minutes, to allow them to char slightly, before stirring again. Add the mushrooms and (bell) pepper and continue to stir fry for 2–3 minutes.

3   Pour very hot water over the yakisoba noodles (from the tap or kettle) and use tongs to wiggle them around and separate them. Add them to the pan and toss through the vegetables. Add the sauce and combine well to coat the noodles. Cook for a further 2 minutes. Remove from the heat, add the spring onions (scallions) and stir well. Top with the nori and pickled ginger, if using.

Chicken Nugget Mazeman

SERVES 2

8 chicken nuggets
1 egg (or 2 if you're hungry)
¼ block Japanese curry block
    (I use Java Curry)
1 tbsp butter
200ml (7fl oz) chicken stock
2 nests ramen noodles
4 tbsp sweetcorn (I use canned)
1 spring onion (scallion),
    finely sliced
1 tbsp furikake

NOTE
This recipe calls for eight nuggets
(purposefully). If you're picking
them up from our friend Ronald,
buy a nine box and treat yourself
to one for the effort of collecting
them. You earned it.

If you know me, you know that I'm partial to the wares of certain golden arches. Especially chicken nuggets. I love them. They're just pure, simple comfort for me. During the first lockdown of 2020, when I heard restaurants would be closing, I went and bought two chick-a-bricks (that's the name for a box of 20 where I come from), and I put them in the freezer. They reheated remarkably well, especially in the air fryer. I've since used them in some rather novel ways – some worked, some didn't. One of my favourites was a chicken nugget bánh-mì-style baguette. Another is these noodles.

Mazeman translates from Japanese as 'mixed noodles'. It's typically served with similar toppings and composition to ramen – roast pork, soft-boiled egg, wood ear mushrooms, bamboo shoots – but without the broth. Here I've combined the noodles and nuggets with a curry sauce, made using a Japanese curry block (a must-have pantry item).

1   You don't have to reheat the nuggets if they're fresh from a takeaway, but if you're cooking nuggets from the freezer, do so now according to the packet instructions.

2   Meanwhile, fill the kettle and boil. Set two pans on the hob. Fill one pan three-quarters full with boiling water and set over a high heat. Once rapidly boiling, lower in the egg(s) and set a timer for 6 minutes 45 seconds. Keep an eye on this timer.

3   In a separate pan, over a medium heat, add the curry block, the butter and chicken stock. Stir quickly with a fork, pressing on the curry block to dissolve until a smooth sauce forms.

4   When the timer has 2 minutes left on the clock, drop in the ramen noodles alongside the egg/s (adjust this time according to the packet instructions). Once the timer pings, pop the egg(s) and noodles into a colander and run the whole lot under cool water for 1 minute. Fish out the egg(s) and peel, when cool enough. Heat the sweetcorn in a small bowl in the microwave for 20 seconds, or add for the final minute of the noodle cooking time.

5   Divide the hot curry sauce between two bowls. Divide the noodles in two and place on top of the sauce. Top this with an egg half (or two), the sliced spring onion (scallion), the sweetcorn and a sprinkle of furikake. Tear up the nuggets and add them on top of the noodles. Toss and enjoy.

Sizzling Red Oil Noodles

SERVES 2 · V

1 tbsp light soy sauce

1 tbsp Chinkiang black rice vinegar

1 tsp golden caster (superfine) sugar

2 nests Taiwanese flower petal noodles or wide wheat noodles

2 heads choi sum or pak choi (bok choy), leaves separated

2 tsp Sichuan ground chilli (red pepper) flakes (see note)

2 spring onions (scallions), finely diced

2 large garlic cloves (or 4 small), grated or crushed

1 tsp toasted sesame seeds

sea salt

3 tbsp neutral oil

2 fried eggs (optional)

NOTE

Be sure to use ground Sichuan chilli (red pepper) flakes for this recipe. These will give the dressing a gorgeous bright red hue and the traditional flavour profile. Gochugaru, Korean red pepper flakes, will also work. Italian chilli (red pepper) flakes will not give the same flavour or colour, so don't be tempted to use them if that's all you have in your cupboard.

The title of this recipe makes it sound very dramatic and theatrical, which it is. Pouring hot oil over the raw ingredients and noodles creates mini fireworks inside the bowl. But the reason I love it the most, is that it's so, so quick. It also only uses one pan, so there's minimal mess.

Yo Po Mian is the name of noodles made using this technique. It originates in Shaanxi province, China, and would typically suit a thicker handmade noodle such as biang biang noodles. To emulate this as best I can, without hand-making the noodles myself, I use the widest of the dried noodles I keep in my pantry – frilly flower petal noodles, from Taiwan. The frills on the edges of the noodles pick up the fragrant oil and gubbins perfectly.

If you want to make this vegan, omit the egg.

1 Combine the light soy sauce, vinegar and sugar in a cup and stir until the sugar dissolves.

2 Bring a pot of boiling salted water to the boil and add the noodles. Cook according to the packet instructions. When there is 1 minute left of cooking time, add the leafy greens. Once cooked, pop the noodles and greens into a colander and rinse with cold water – this keeps the noodles springy and stops them clumping together.

3 Divide the noodles and greens between two bowls. On top, in small separate piles, add the chilli (red pepper) flakes, spring onions (scallions), grated garlic, sesame seeds and a pinch of sea salt.

4 Move your bowls close to the hob, so you aren't carrying a hot pan of oil across the kitchen. Heat the neutral oil in a small pan over a high heat until it's smoking. This may seem a little daunting, and be sure to use caution, but you do want it to be hot enough to see smoke rising. Once hot enough, immediately pour the oil over the two little collections of aromatics on top of the noodles, half over each. The oil should splutter a little, as it hits the wet ingredients and cooks the garlic.

5 Divide the soy sauce mixture between the two bowls, and toss everything together. I love to serve this with a simple fried egg on top, if I'm in the mood, but it's just as good without.

Creamy, Umami Lap Cheong Spaghetti

SERVES 2

120g (4¼oz) bronze-cut spaghetti
4 egg yolks
1 tbsp white miso
60g (2¼oz) freshly, finely grated
  parmesan
½ tsp freshly ground black pepper
1 tbsp olive oil
1 lap cheong, diced (or thick-cut
  pancetta)
1 tbsp furikake

I love carbonara. It's so quick and easy to put together. I craved it when I was pregnant with my first child and would get out of bed post-midnight to cook it! This version came into being when I had one such hankering but had no pancetta or bacon (the traditional version uses guanciale, cured pig's cheek) in the fridge. I did, however, have some lap cheong, a dried Chinese sausage, which comes in a variety of flavours, and sometimes includes liver. I usually have plain pork flavour. It's also delicious steamed atop rice and worked really well to curb my carbonara cravings.

When it comes to pasta, bronze-cut spaghetti is always my preference. The rough texture allows the sauce to cling to it better, but if you can't find it, regular spaghetti will work well, too.

While the below is in no way an authentic carbonara, it follows the same principles – fatty, salty meat; creamy, cheesy, umami sauce and slippery spaghetti.

1   Cook the spaghetti according to the packet instructions, or until al dente. While it's cooking, add the egg yolks to a large mixing bowl along with the miso, parmesan and black pepper. Mix well until it forms a thick paste.

2   Heat the oil in a non-stick, heavy-based frying pan (skillet) and add the lap cheong. Stir fry for 1–2 minutes or until it's beginning to crisp and some of the fat has rendered.

3   Once the spaghetti is cooked, transfer it directly into the pan with the lap cheong, using tongs, and let it soak up some of the fat. Reserve the pasta water. Remove the pan from the heat and let it cool slightly for 3–4 minutes (you don't want to add the spaghetti to the egg mix while it is scorching hot, or it will scramble the eggs).

4   Add the spaghetti to the mixing bowl along with 2 tbsp of the pasta cooking water and mix until each spaghetti strand is coated in glossy sauce. Serve sprinkled with furikake.

Spicy Egg Noodles

SERVES 2 · V

2 tbsp neutral oil

4 eggs, beaten

2 spring onions (scallions), sliced
into 1cm (½in) rounds

2 garlic cloves, grated or crushed

1 red chilli, sliced, plus extra to
serve (optional)

1 green chilli, sliced

1 tbsp light soy sauce

1 tsp dark soy sauce

1 tbsp mushroom stir fry sauce

2 tbsp soy bean sauce

1 tsp light (soft) brown sugar

1 tsp mushroom bouillon powder

100ml (3½oz) vegetable stock

2 nests thick wheat noodles

1 tsp toasted sesame oil

This recipe is fast and makes the most of store-cupboard ingredients. You stir scrambled eggs into the sauce, which is a method I just can't quit. If you've never tried it, rectify that immediately.

1   Heat 1 tbsp of the oil in a non-stick, heavy-based frying pan (skillet) over a low-medium heat, add the eggs and scramble until just set. Remove from the pan and set aside.

2   Give the pan a quick wipe, add the remaining tbsp of oil and turn the heat up to medium-high. Add the spring onions (scallions), garlic and chillies and fry until fragrant but not coloured. Add the light soy, dark soy, mushroom stir fry sauce, soy bean sauce, sugar, mushroom bouillon powder and vegetable stock. Stir and let it bubble gently for 2–3 minutes. Add the scrambled eggs back into the sauce and stir to combine. Leave the pan on a very low heat while you cook the noodles.

3   Cook the noodles according to the packet instructions. Strain and rinse under cool water, separating the noodles with your fingers, to prevent them from sticking. Add the sesame oil to the noodles and toss to coat. Serve the eggy sauce on top of the noodles and garnish with more fresh red chilli, if desired.

Soba with Roasted Greens

SERVES 4 · VG

200g (7oz) long-stemmed
  broccoli
100g (3½oz) asparagus, chopped
  into 5cm (2in) pieces
100g (3½oz) spring onion
  (scallion), chopped into 5cm
  (2in) pieces
½ garlic head, unpeeled
6 tbsp olive oil
140g (5oz) coriander (cilantro),
  reserving a few sprigs to serve
2 large green chillies
1 tbsp golden caster (superfine)
  sugar
½ tsp sea salt
juice of 2 limes
4 nests soba noodles
1 handful of frozen peas
4 tbsp Sichuan chilli oil or Lao Gan
  Ma Crispy Chilli Oil
2 tbsp toasted sesame seeds

Earlier this year I succumbed to the temptation of buying an air fryer, despite being very precious about my counter-top space.

My favourite thing to cook in the air fryer is green veg, especially broccoli. It gives it a delicious, nutty, roasted char in less than 10 minutes. And my favourite thing about this recipe is that it can be served hot or cold and it comes together in less than 15 minutes.

If you don't have an air fryer, just roast the veg in the oven – it takes slightly longer but will taste just as great.

1   Preheat the oven to 200°C/180°C fan/400°F/gas mark 6, if you don't have an air fryer.

2   Lay the veg and garlic out on a chopping board and drizzle with 2 tbsp of the olive oil. Rub to coat. Wrap the garlic in foil, then place everything into the air fryer and roast for 8 minutes, giving everything a toss halfway through. If you don't have an air fryer, roast in the oven for 20 minutes. The veg should be nice and charred and the garlic should be softened and squishy.

3   In a high-speed blender, whizz the coriander (cilantro), chillies, sugar, salt, lime juice, roasted garlic cloves (skin removed) and the remaining 4 tbsp olive oil to a smooth green sauce.

4   Cook the soba noodles and the peas in boiling water for 4 minutes (or according to the packet instructions), strain and rinse under cool water, separating the noodles with your fingers, to prevent them from sticking.

5   To serve, spread the green sauce out onto a serving platter. Add the noodles and peas, and pile the roasted green veg on top. Drizzle everything with crispy chilli oil and sprinkle with the toasted sesame seeds and coriander leaves.

Bangkok-style Spaghetti

SERVES 4

240g (8½oz) bronze-cut spaghetti
3 tbsp Thai seasoning sauce
2 tbsp Thai oyster sauce
2 tsp dark soy sauce
1½ tbsp golden caster (superfine)
   sugar
1 tsp garlic salt
3 tbsp butter
1 tbsp neutral oil
6 anchovies, chopped
6 garlic cloves, grated or crushed
24 frozen king prawns (jumbo
   shrimp), defrosted
1 red onion, sliced
1 red (bell) pepper, sliced
2–4 red bird's eye chillies,
   finely sliced
1 handful of picked Thai basil
   leaves
2 tsp freshly ground black pepper

Italian-Thai fusion is not a new phenomenon and became popular shortly after the Vietnam War with the arrival of American troops and, later, tourists. Pizza and pasta, especially macaroni, were cooked with classic Thai flavours, such as lemongrass, lime, bird's eye chilli and garlic, and became a mainstay in Bangkok before spreading to the rest of the country.

Spaghetti Kee Mao is one such dish, where spaghetti is used in place of rice noodles in Pad Kee Mao, also known as drunken noodles. I first tried this dish in a Bangkok mall in 2019 – I'm a sucker for spaghetti and I love the aforementioned Thai seasonings, so this dish spoke to my heart.

One of my favourite recipes for this style of pasta comes from Kris Yenbamroong's book *Night + Market*, which utilizes the novel addition of pink peppercorns.

For my recipe, at a pinch, you could use linguine instead of spaghetti and frozen squid rings work well in place of prawns (shrimp).

1   Cook the spaghetti in a pan of boiling, salted water for 8–10 minutes or until al dente, depending on its thickness.

2   Meanwhile, mix the Thai seasoning sauce, oyster sauce, dark soy, sugar and garlic salt in a cup or jug (pitcher), to make the sauce. Set aside.

3   When the pasta is around 5 minutes away from al dente, add the butter and oil to a non-stick, heavy-based frying pan (skillet) and set over a medium heat. Add the anchovies and garlic and keep them moving for 2 minutes. The garlic will become fragrant and the anchovies should dissolve.

4   Add the king prawns (jumbo shrimp) and stir fry for 2–3 minutes, until just turning pink. Add the onion, (bell) pepper and chillies. Stir fry for 2–3 minutes, keeping everything moving to prevent burning.

5   Put the pasta, straight from its pan, in with the stir-fried prawns and vegetables. Add the sauce and combine well. Remove from the heat and sprinkle over the Thai basil and black pepper.

Stay-at-home Beef Ho Fun

SERVES 2

1 tsp cornflour (cornstarch)
4 tbsp light soy sauce
1 bavette (flank) or sirloin steak, thinly sliced against the grain
1 tbsp dark soy sauce
1 tsp golden caster (superfine) sugar
1 tsp toasted sesame oil
400g (14oz) fresh wide rice (ho fun) noodles
4 tbsp neutral oil
1 small onion, sliced
3 spring onions (scallions), finely shredded
2 handfuls of bean sprouts

I've called this dish 'Stay-at-home' Ho Fun, because to achieve that distinctive restaurant-style Beef Ho Fun flavour, you really need wok hei (see page 21). Wok hei creates those beautiful smoky, charred layers of flavour. It's really difficult to accomplish wok hei at home – ideally you need a high-powered wok burner to create the high temperatures needed. Some chefs suggest using a blowtorch or other inventive methods, but I neither have the tools or the time for these. If I want the real deal, I order from my local Chinese restaurant. Here's how I make it at home.

1   Combine the cornflour (cornstarch), 1 tbsp of the light soy sauce with 1 tsp water in a bowl. Add the beef and mix well until the slices are coated in the slurry. Leave this for 5 minutes, while you prep the vegetables and noodles.

2   In another bowl or jug (pitcher), add the remaining 3 tbsp light soy, the dark soy, sugar and sesame oil to make the sauce. Stir until the sugar is dissolved. Set aside.

3   Bring a pan of water to the boil and cook the noodles for 20–30 seconds, or until they begin to separate (when using fresh rice noodles, they can sometimes stick together in the packet). Drain and rinse under cool water, separating the noodles with your fingers, to prevent them from sticking again. Set aside.

4   Heat 2 tbsp of the neutral oil in a non-stick, heavy-based frying pan (skillet) or wok. Add the marinated beef and let it sit for a few minutes in the pan to fry until crispy and brown. Remove from the pan and set aside. Wipe the pan and set it back over the heat.

5   Add the remaining 2 tbsp oil to the pan and heat until the pan is smoking and the oil is shimmering. Add the onion and toss quickly for 2 minutes – you want to create blackened edges on the onions and keep them crisp. Add the noodles and toss through, before allowing them to sit and also pick up some char. Add the beef back into the pan, along with the spring onions (scallions) and bean sprouts. Toss to combine.

6   Add the sauce and stir well until all the noodles are coated and the sauce has been absorbed. Serve immediately.

Soy Garlic Butter Prawn Spaghetti

SERVES 2 (OR 1, IF YOU'RE ANYTHING LIKE ME)

120g (4¼oz) bronze-cut spaghetti
3 tbsp salted butter
1 tbsp olive oil
3 garlic cloves, crushed or grated
8–10 large frozen king prawns
   (jumbo shrimp), defrosted
1 courgette (zucchini), chopped
   into 4cm (1½in) batons
1 tsp garlic salt or sea salt
½ tsp freshly ground black pepper
2 tbsp light soy sauce
1 tsp dark soy sauce

Of all the recipes in this book, this is the one I have probably made the most this year. Inspired by the Italian classic Spaghetti Gamberetti, which combines pasta and prawns (shrimp), it has an added layer of seasoning from the soy sauces. I have actually just finished a bowl and it is sitting, empty, next to my laptop right now as I debate in my head whether to text my partner, from upstairs, to ask him to put some more spaghetti on because I want another bowl.

I think the reason I make this so often is because it takes little more than 5 minutes of hands-on cooking time. It's also extremely tasty and moreish, as my current dilemma proves.

It works really well with roasted long-stemmed broccoli and squid rings, too.

1   Bring a large pan of salted water to the boil. Drop in the spaghetti and cook according to the packet instructions or until al dente. Once the pasta is cooked, turn off the heat, but leave it in the pan with its cooking water.

2   Meanwhile, set a non-stick, heavy-based frying pan (skillet) over a high heat and add the butter, olive oil and garlic. Once the butter has melted and the garlic has become fragrant, 1–2 minutes, add the king prawns (jumbo shrimp). Fry for 2 minutes or until they just turn pink, then add the courgette (zucchini) batons. Season with the salt and pepper and keep everything moving quickly so that nothing burns.

3   After 3–4 minutes, the prawns should be cooked. Add the light soy and dark soy. While the pan is still over the heat, transfer the spaghetti from the pan it was cooked in, into the prawn pan, using a pair of tongs. Transferring it this way will ensure some of the starchy pasta water comes with the spaghetti, which will contribute to the luscious sauce. Toss the pasta in the garlicky soy butter and let it soak up all the goodness – the sauce should look slick and golden and cling to the pasta. Serve immediately.

Vegan Fridge-raid Noodles

SERVES 2 · V

2 portions somen noodles or thin
   wheat noodles
1 tbsp neutral oil
2 garlic cloves, grated

For the sauce
2 tbsp light soy sauce
1 tbsp vegetarian oyster sauce
1 tbsp maple syrup
1 tbsp Chinkiang black rice vinegar
2 tbsp Sichuan chilli oil or Lao Gan
   Ma Crispy Chilli Oil

**200–300g (7–10½oz) of any
combination of the following:**
carrot, finely shredded
long-stemmed or regular broccoli
   or broccoli stalks, halved and
   blanched
green beans, trimmed
mushrooms, quartered
baby corn, halved
mange tout (snow peas)
choi sum or pak choi (bok choy),
   leaves separated
(bell) pepper, finely shredded
cabbage leaves, finely sliced
bean sprouts

With one of any of the following:
½ red onion, sliced
2–3 spring onions (scallions),
   chopped into 2.5cm (1in) pieces

**So often, I have half a courgette (zucchini), half a carrot and some
wilting greens knocking around in my fridge. I hate throwing food
away, and this recipe is a perfectly quick and satisfying way to use it
up, that is quick and easy. It can be adapted to the seasons and truly
is hard to get wrong.**

**You can double or triple the sauce and keep it in a sterilized airtight
jar with a lid for up to 3 weeks in the fridge, to save even more time.
The addition of leftover chicken or roast meat works really well, too.**

1   Cook the noodles according to the packet instructions. Drain and rinse
    under cool water, separating the noodles with your fingers, to prevent
    them from sticking.

2   Combine the light soy, oyster sauce, maple syrup, Chinkiang black rice
    vinegar and chilli oil in a jug (pitcher) to make the sauce. Set aside.

3   Heat the neutral oil in a non-stick, heavy-based frying pan (skillet) or
    wok, set over a medium-high heat. Add the garlic and fry for 30 seconds
    until fragrant.

4   Add your chosen vegetables in two lots, beginning with the most fibrous
    (e.g. carrots, broccoli, green beans, mushrooms, baby corn). Stir fry
    for 2–3 minutes, until the veg begins to soften. Add the second lot of
    vegetables, e.g. mange tout (snow peas), pak choi (bok choy), (bell)
    pepper, cabbage and bean sprouts, along with the onion or spring onion
    (scallion). Continue to stir fry for 2 minutes, keeping everything moving
    around the pan.

5   Add the noodles, followed by the sauce and toss to coat everything
    well, for 1–2 minutes, until the noodles and sauce are heated through.
    Serve immediately.

Quick-sharp Dan Dan Mian

SERVES 2

2 tbsp Chinese sesame paste
    or tahini
1 tbsp peanut butter
2 tbsp light soy sauce
1 tbsp Chinkiang black rice vinegar
2 tsp light (soft) brown sugar
2 tbsp Sichuan chilli oil or Lao Gan
    Ma Crispy Chilli Oil
1 tbsp neutral oil
200g (7oz) fatty beef mince
    (ground beef)
1 tsp Chinese five spice
3 tbsp hoisin sauce
1 tsp dark soy sauce
2 nests thin wheat noodles
100ml (3½oz) hot chicken stock
1 spring onion (scallion), diced

If you know me, you know that Dan Dan Mian is one of my all-time favourites. You can find many versions and styles of this dish at different restaurants, and there are just as many recipes. There are several different iterations I will use myself at home – from preparing the noodles, stock and chilli oil by hand, to a 20-minute version using store-bought stock and non-traditional ingredients, such as pickles and peanut butter.

This quick-sharp Dan Dan Mian is my bare-bones version, without any frills or additional extras. If you have some ya cai (Sichuan pickled mustard greens) in your cupboards, I would always add some to this dish, just at the end.

1   Combine the sesame paste, peanut butter, light soy sauce, rice vinegar, sugar and chilli oil in a high-speed blender, or in a jug (pitcher) using a stick blender, to make the sauce. Set aside.

2   Heat the neutral oil in a non-stick, heavy-based frying pan (skillet) and add the beef mince. Let this sit for 2–3 minutes in the hot pan, without stirring, to allow it to brown. Add the Chinese five spice and stir fry for another 2–3 minutes until the beef is browned all over. Add the hoisin sauce and dark soy, and mix well until the mince is coated and glossy.

3   Meanwhile, cook the noodles according to the packet instructions.

4   Divide the sauce between two bowls, top up with the hot stock and combine well. Add the noodles and top with the beef and diced spring onion (scallion).

Fried Egg Noodles

SERVES 2 · V

2 garlic cloves, grated

2 red bird's eye chillies, sliced

2 tbsp fish sauce

3 tbsp lime juice

3 tsp golden caster (superfine) sugar

2 tbsp Maggi Liquid Seasoning

1 tsp dark soy sauce

2 nests dried lo mein thick egg noodles

2 tbsp neutral oil

4 eggs

1 shallot, finely sliced

1 handful of coriander (cilantro), roughly chopped

I was once asked 'Do you put a fried egg on everything?', which is a great question because I put fried eggs on a lot of things. I especially love putting them onto my noodles. Eggs are just great. They're quick, versatile and a good source of protein. It's one thing I really hate running out of – and something I'm willing to go to the supermarket on the other side of town at 11pm for.

The Thai dish Yam Khai Dao is one of my favourite ways to eat eggs. It's a fried egg salad with fried eggs chopped up and served with shallots and coriander (cilantro), and perked up with a punchy lime, fish sauce and chilli dressing. It's great as a side dish or served with rice (one of my favourite ways to eat it). And, as it turns out, egg noodles. This version uses Maggi, garlic and dark soy sauce to turn it into a noodle sauce rather than a dressing and it really hits the spot.

1   Mix the garlic, chillies, fish sauce, lime juice, sugar, Maggi Liquid Seasoning and dark soy in a jug (pitcher), stirring until the sugar dissolves, to make the dressing. Set aside.

2   Cook the noodles according to the packet instructions or until al dente. Drain and rinse under cool water, separating the noodles with your fingers, to prevent them from sticking. Set aside.

3   Heat 1 tbsp of the neutral oil in a non-stick, heavy-based frying pan (skillet) over a medium heat, and crack in the 4 eggs. It's okay if they overlap. Leave them to cook gently until the edges become crispy and the yolks are half set and slightly runny. Remove the eggs from the pan and cut them up into 5cm (2in) pieces – I use kitchen scissors for this.

4   While the pan is still hot, add the noodles and toss through the remaining 1 tbsp oil. Add the eggs back in and then add the dressing. Stir fry quickly for 3–4 minutes until the noodles are hot.

5   Remove from the heat and divide into two bowls. Top with the shallots and coriander (cilantro).

Unagi Soba

SERVES 2

¼ cucumber, finely sliced
1 tbsp fine sea salt
1 tbsp golden caster (superfine) sugar
2 tsp toasted sesame oil
1 tbsp Japanese soy sauce
1 tsp maple syrup
1 x 200g (7oz) frozen unagi kabayaki
1 egg
1 generous handful of frozen edamame beans
2 nests dried soba noodles
1 tbsp furikake

Unagi is freshwater eel and in Japanese cuisine it is commonly served as kabayaki – the fish is split and butterflied, arranged on skewers, dressed with a sweet soy glaze and grilled or barbecued, which gives it a beautifully sweet and smoky flavour. Unagi is commonly served on top of sushi rice and it's one of my favourite things to order at Japanese restaurants, or when ordering sushi at home.

You can buy prepared kabayaki from the freezer section of East and Southeast Asian supermarkets (I use Yutaka) and it's ideal for a simple meal, served on top of rice for unadon, with some simple pickled cucumbers or, as here, atop soba noodles.

1   Add the finely sliced cucumber to a sieve (strainer) set over the sink and add the salt and sugar. Mix well to coat the cucumber. Leave it while you prepare the rest of the dish.

2   Combine the sesame oil, soy sauce and maple syrup in a jug (pitcher) to make the dressing. Set aside.

3   Bring a large pan of water to the boil. Add the frozen unagi, in its packaging (boil-in-the-bag style) and cook for 6 minutes. Carefully remove the packet from the water and set aside to cool.

4   Bring the water back to the boil and drop in the egg and edamame beans. Set a timer for 6 minutes 30 seconds. After 2 minutes, drop in the soba noodles. When the timer alarms, pop everything into a colander. Pluck out the egg and set aside to cool. Return the soba and edamame to the pan. Add the sauce and toss through.

5   Divide the noodles and edamame between two bowls. Peel the egg and cut it in half. Set each half on top of the soba noodles. Cut open the packet of eel and divide between the two bowls.

6   Briefly rinse the cucumbers to get rid of any excess salt and sugar, and squeeze them in your fist to get rid of any excess moisture. They should crinkle in your hand. Arrange on top of the soba noodles, garnish with a liberal sprinkling of furikake and serve.

Ham and Green Eggs Noodles

SERVES 2

4 eggs
100g (3½oz) cavolo nero or kale,
    tough stems removed, finely
    shredded
1 spring onion (scallion), sliced
2 tbsp neutral oil
2 tbsp butter
1 garlic clove, crushed or grated
100g (3½oz) pork belly slices,
    chopped into 1cm (½in) pieces
2 nests fresh or dried thick
    wheat noodles
1 handful of frozen peas
1 tbsp light soy sauce
1 tbsp kecap manis
¼ tsp freshly ground black pepper

This recipe is another family favourite and one of my many attempts to make my daughters' meals fun and interesting. Adding the ingredients to the eggs and beating them together is an achievable task for little hands.

I often swap out the pork belly for smoked bacon or Chinese air-dried ham, depending on what I have in the fridge at the time. It also works really well with crumbled sausage meat.

1   Beat the eggs in a deep bowl and add the shredded cavolo nero and spring onion (scallion).

2   Heat 1 tbsp of the neutral oil in a non-stick, heavy-based frying pan (skillet) over a medium-high heat and spread it around the pan using paper towel. Add the egg mixture and swirl the pan to create a thin omelette. Cook on both sides for 1–2 minutes, until the eggs are just set. Transfer from the pan to a chopping board and, when cool enough, roll it up into a sausage shape. Cut the omelette into 1cm (½in) slices and set aside.

3   Wipe the pan, return to a medium heat and add the remaining 1 tbsp of neutral oil, the butter and garlic. Fry for 30 seconds, until fragrant. Add the pork belly and cook on all sides for 3–4 minutes, until evenly browned and crispy.

4   Meanwhile, cook the noodles according to the packet instructions.

5   Add the peas to the pork and cook for another minute. Add the light soy sauce, kecap manis and black pepper and mix well. Scoop the noodles from their pan and pop them straight into the frying pan (skillet) with the pork and peas. Fold through the buttery soy sauce. Add the omelette pieces and toss through. Serve immediately.

Hot and Sour Red Oil Broth

SERVES 2

2 tbsp dried, shredded black
    fungus mushrooms
1 egg
2 nests thin wheat noodles
1 head of pak choi (bok choy), cut
    in half, stem removed
1 tsp toasted sesame oil
2 garlic cloves, grated or crushed
2 spring onions (scallions),
    finely chopped
2 tbsp toasted sesame seeds
2 tbsp Sichuan chilli (red pepper)
    flakes or gochugaru
4 tbsp neutral oil
2 tbsp light soy sauce
2 tbsp Chinkiang black rice vinegar
1 tbsp oyster sauce
1 tsp chicken or mushroom
    bouillon powder
½ tsp sea salt
1 tsp light (soft) brown sugar
1 small handful of coriander
    (cilantro), roughly chopped

One of the quickest ways to make a delicious, fragrant sauce, with minimal washing up, is to add the chopped aromatics – garlic, spring onion (scallion), chilli (red pepper) flakes, sesame seeds – to a bowl and pour over smoking hot oil, this technique is what inspired my Sizzling Red Oil Noodles (see page 58). The oil quickly cooks the aromatics, releasing a burst of fragrance into the air, while also creating a snap, crackle and pop, and this technique can also be used to create a very quick and inviting broth.

Yo Po Mian – the dish famed for this technique – originates in Shaanxi province, China, and would typically use thicker handmade noodles, such as biang biang noodles.

Be sure to use Sichuan chilli (red pepper) flakes, or at a pinch, gochugaru. These chilli flakes will create the beautiful red colour that we want. Sichuan flakes are much spicier than gochugaru, as they are made from different chillies, so tailor to your own taste.

1   Rehydrate the black fungus mushrooms in a mug of boiling water for 10 minutes.

2   Bring a large pan of water to the boil. Drop in the egg and set a timer for 6 minutes 45 seconds. When there is 5 minutes remaining on the timer (or, after the time stated on the noodle packet), add the noodles. When there is 4 minutes remaining, add the pak choi (bok choy). When the time is up, pop everything into a colander and rinse under cool water. Pick out the egg, peel and set aside. Pick out the pak choi (bok choy) and set aside. Add the toasted sesame oil to the noodles and toss to coat. Set aside.

3   Into the centre of two large, deep bowls, add the garlic, spring onions (scallions), sesame seeds and chilli (red pepper) flakes in 4 distinct piles, so each can be clearly seen and neither is buried underneath another.

4   Heat the neutral oil until it reaches smoking point. Pour 2 tbsp of the hot oil over each pile of aromatics. This will spit and bubble a little. Once cooled, to each bowl add 1 tbsp light soy, 1 tbsp rice vinegar, ½ tbsp oyster sauce, ½ tsp bouillon powder, ¼ tsp sea salt, ½ tsp sugar and 150ml (5fl oz) freshly boiled water from a kettle. Stir until combined.

5   To the bowls of broth, add the noodles, pak choi (bok choy), half an egg and the soaked black fungus, then top with coriander (cilantro).

Coconut Curry Noodles

SERVES 2

1 tbsp neutral oil

2 tbsp Thai red or green
curry paste

200ml (7fl oz) chicken bone broth
or vegetable stock

2 tbsp fish sauce or soy sauce

2 tsp light (soft) brown sugar

400ml (14fl oz) tin coconut milk

2 nests dried egg noodles or
yellow noodles

1 small courgette (zucchini)

1 handful of bean sprouts

1 handful of leftover roast chicken
or 6 tofu puffs, halved

1 small handful of coriander
(cilantro), roughly chopped

½ red onion, finely sliced

1 large red chilli, finely sliced

1 lime, cut into 4

I adore the fresh, bright, zingy, spicy flavours of Thai food, and this is my nod to them. Having a tub of Thai curry paste in the fridge is always a saving grace when I'm after a quick and easy meal midweek. If you don't have leftover chicken, you could use frozen prawns or squid. You can also make this vegan, just make sure the curry paste is vegan-friendly and use thin, yellow, eggless noodles.

1 Heat the neutral oil in a large pan over a medium heat. Add the curry paste and fry for 30 seconds–1 minute or until fragrant. Add the broth, fish sauce and sugar and mix well. Taste and adjust the seasonings as necessary. Add the coconut milk and bring to a gentle simmer.

2 Meanwhile, cook the noodles in a separate pan of boiling water, according to the packet instructions.

3 Using a vegetable peeler, peel the courgette (zucchini) into ribbons. Drop the courgette (zucchini), bean sprouts and chicken (or tofu) into the hot broth and cook for 1–2 minutes.

4 Serve the broth over the noodles and garnish with coriander (cilantro), red onion, chilli and a good squeeze of lime juice.

Freezer Wonton Noodle Soup

SERVES 2

12 frozen prawn wontons

2 nests fresh Hong Kong wonton noodles or thin egg noodles

600ml (21fl oz) chicken bone broth or stock

3 tbsp oyster sauce

1 tbsp light soy sauce

1 tsp fish sauce

2 tsp light (soft) brown sugar

1 tbsp toasted sesame oil

2 spring onions (scallions), greens finely sliced

Alongside the drawer full of freezer dumplings that I eat in ramen, broths or on their own, is a multitude of frozen dim sum – cheung fun, siu mai, har gau (steamed buns) – and wontons. The latter are perfect on their own or for making a super-quick version of Cantonese wonton noodle soup. They cook straight from frozen in around the same time it takes to heat some broth and cook some noodles, which means, with a little forethought, this dish can come together in less than 15 minutes. (See page 23 for my favourite brand.)

1   Bring a large pan of water to the boil. Drop in the frozen wontons and cook for the time stated on the packet. Set a timer and drop in the wonton noodles when the timer reads the correct cooking time for the noodles.

2   In a separate pan, heat the bone broth until steaming. Season with the oyster sauce, light soy sauce, fish sauce, sugar and sesame oil. Combine well and adjust the seasonings if necessary. Decant into two large bowls.

3   When the noodles and wontons are ready, remove from the heat and transfer the noodles into the hot broth. Scoop out the wontons and sit them on top of the noodles. Garnish with the spring onion (scallion) greens and serve immediately so the noodles don't become soggy.

Quick Garlic Miso Ramen

SERVES 2

2 tbsp neutral oil
2 garlic cloves, grated or crushed
2.5cm (1in) ginger, peeled
   and grated
600ml (21fl oz) chicken bone
   broth
3 tbsp white miso
4 tbsp oat milk
2 tbsp light soy sauce
2 tbsp mirin
¼ tsp freshly ground black pepper
200g (7oz) fatty pork mince
   (ground pork)
2 tbsp soy bean sauce
1 tsp dark soy sauce
1 egg
2 nests fresh or dried ramen
   noodles
1 handful of bean sprouts
1 small leek, finely shredded
½ toasted nori sheet, cut into 4
1 tbsp furikake

While investing your time in a 3-hour broth is almost always certainly worth it (see my book *Bowls & Broths* if you like the sound of that), when I'm time poor, my need for a steaming bowl of ramen doesn't dissipate. As with all bowls of broth, a bowl of ramen is only as good as the base stock it's made with. Most supermarkets have great ones and I find that the broths that come in bags, in the fridge section, will have more body and substance than stock cubes. If you can find bone broth, even better, as this will be packed with the collagen and fats that we need to make a good bowl of ramen in limited time. You can also order decent bone broths online (see page 165).

1   Heat 1 tbsp of the neutral oil in a pan over a medium-high heat. Add the garlic and ginger and stir fry for 30 seconds, until fragrant. Add the chicken bone broth and stir to combine. Bring the stock to a gentle simmer and add the miso paste, oat milk, light soy sauce, mirin and pepper. Stir with a whisk or fork until the miso paste dissolves (you can use a stick blender to speed up the process – just be careful of hot stock splattering). Leave to gently simmer over a low heat.

2   Bring a large saucepan of water to the boil, ready to cook the noodles.

3   Meanwhile, heat the remaining 1 tbsp neutral oil in a non-stick, heavy-based frying pan (skillet) over a high heat. Add the pork mince and fry for 3–4 minutes until browned and crispy on all sides. Add the soy bean sauce and dark soy sauce, with a splash of noodle cooking water. Mix well with the pork and leave over a low heat.

4   Drop the egg into the boiling water. Set a timer for 6 minutes 45 seconds. After 2 minutes or so, add the ramen noodles and cook for the time stated on the packet. With 1 minute remaining on the clock, add the bean sprouts.

5   Strain and divide the noodles and bean sprouts between two bowls. Pluck out the egg and allow to cool slightly before peeling and halving.

6   Pour the hot broth over the noodles in each bowl and top with the pork mixture, half an egg, the leek, nori and furikake.

Fuss-Free Noodles

20+ MINUTES

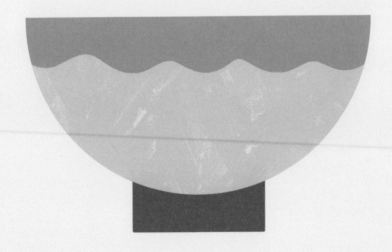

Non-nuclear Fire Noodles

SERVES 2

1 tbsp gochujang

1 tbsp sriracha (or your favourite fruity hot sauce)

½ tbsp chicken bouillon powder

1 garlic clove, grated

½ tbsp light soy sauce

½ tbsp golden caster (superfine) sugar

½ tbsp toasted sesame oil

2 nests ramen noodles (fresh or dried)

1 tbsp neutral oil

2 boneless chicken thighs, finely sliced

2 spring onions (scallions), finely sliced

2 egg yolks (optional)

½ toasted nori sheet, torn into small pieces

1 tbsp crispy fried garlic

Buldak Nuclear Fire Noodles are the best-selling instant noodles from Korean brand Samyang and have something of a cult following. TikTokers and YouTubers began taking on the challenge of eating a bowl of these spicy noodles and recording their sweaty, nose-dribbling demise. What keeps them all coming back for more, though, is that despite the heat (4,404 Scoville units, to be precise), the noodles are moreishly tasty. While this extreme level of heat is not something I crave, the spicy, chickeny flavour definitely is. And so these are the building blocks of this dish.

I love adding a raw egg yolk to the centre as the heat from the noodles cooks the yolk and it adds a lovely creaminess. If you'd rather, you could always fry the egg. If you want to make this vegan, omit the egg and switch the chicken bouillon for mushroom bouillon powder.

1   Mix the gochujang, sriracha, chicken bouillon powder, grated garlic, light soy, sugar and sesame oil together in a jug (pitcher).

2   Bring a pot of water to the boil and cook the noodles according to the packet instructions. Add 4 tbsp of the noodle water to the jug, then strain the noodles and rinse with cool water, separating the noodles with your fingers, to prevent them from sticking. Set aside.

3   Heat the oil in a non-stick, heavy-based frying pan (skillet). Add the chicken pieces and sear on all sides. Once sealed, pour in the sauce from the jug and allow it to bubble away for 2–3 minutes or until the chicken is just cooked through. Add the noodles and spring onions (scallions), tossing to coat.

4   Divide the noodles between two bowls. Make a little dent in the middle of each and plop in an egg yolk, if using. Sprinkle with the torn nori and crispy garlic and serve immediately.

Peggy's Noodles

SERVES 2 ADULTS AND 1 TODDLER

2 tbsp light soy sauce

1 tbsp toasted sesame oil

1 tsp maple syrup

1 small carrot, sliced into rounds
(or stars)

3 nests dried soba noodles

1 handful of peas (or sweetcorn)

1 tbsp olive oil

2 tbsp butter

2 garlic cloves, crushed or grated

300g (10½oz) chestnut (cremini)
mushrooms, quartered

14 frozen king prawns (jumbo
shrimp), defrosted

When my daughter Peggy started weaning, I bought little shape cutters to keep her engaged and entertained at mealtimes – they're so fun! Kids are able to use them when supervised and it increased her interest in different fruits and vegetables.

Peg's favourite noodles, by far, are soba noodles, and that's pleasing for me as they only take 4 minutes to cook. She also absolutely loves prawns, but I appreciate this may not be the case for all toddlers, so feel free to switch out proteins as you see fit. And, to make it fun, I serve the dressing in a small measuring spoon on the side of the plate, so she can dress her own dinner.

1   Combine the light soy sauce, sesame oil and maple syrup to make the sauce. Set aside.

2   Bring a pan of water to the boil and drop in the carrot rounds (or stars) and cook for 10 minutes or until soft. When there is approximately 4–5 minutes of cooking time left, add the noodles. When there is 2 minutes of cooking time remaining, drop in the peas. Strain and set aside.

3   In a non-stick, heavy-based frying pan (skillet), over a medium-high heat, heat the olive oil and butter. Fry the garlic for 30 seconds, until fragrant. Add the mushrooms and fry for 3–4 minutes or until evenly browned on all sides. Add the prawns (shrimp) and cook for a further 3–4 minutes until they're pink and cooked through. Reduce the heat and add the noodles/peas/carrots mixture, tossing well.

4   Add the sauce to the pan and toss well to coat. Or, alternatively, serve the dressing on the side for your little one to season their noodles themselves!

King Prawn Lo Mein

SERVES 2

2 nests fresh or dried egg noodles

3 tbsp light soy sauce

2 tbsp oyster sauce

1 tbsp dark soy sauce

½ tbsp golden caster (superfine) sugar

½ tbsp toasted sesame oil

2 tbsp neutral oil

2 garlic cloves, grated or sliced

10 frozen king prawns (jumbo shrimp), defrosted

1 tbsp Shaoxing rice wine

1 small carrot, finely shredded

1 handful of choi sum or pak choi (bok choy), chopped

1 handful of bean sprouts

6 spring onions (scallions), shredded

Lo mein noodles are boiled, then added to cooked vegetables and sauce and tossed through. It's important to have all the veg ready to go, so that the dish comes together quickly and nothing overcooks. This is the kind of dish that, once you've made it once, your process will become streamlined.

1   Cook the noodles according to the packet instructions or until al dente. Strain and rinse under cool water, separating the noodles with your fingers, to prevent them from sticking. Set aside.

2   Meanwhile, combine the light soy, oyster sauce, dark soy, sugar and sesame oil in a small bowl or jug (pitcher), to make the sauce. Set aside.

3   Heat the neutral oil in a non-stick, heavy-based frying pan (skillet) or wok, over a medium-high heat, and add the garlic. Stir it immediately to prevent it burning, cook for 20 seconds, then add the king prawns (jumbo shrimp). Stir fry for 2 minutes, until they're just pink. Add the Shaoxing rice wine and let the alcohol bubble away for 1 minute. Add the carrot and choi sum and continue to stir fry for 3–4 minutes. Add the noodles and the sauce and toss well to combine with the vegetables. The noodles should be coated in sauce.

4   Add the bean sprouts and cook for another minute, before removing the pan from the heat. Add the spring onions (scallions) and serve.

Beef and Broccoli Noodles

SERVES 2

1 tbsp cornflour (cornstarch)
1 tbsp light soy sauce
1 rump steak, thinly sliced
½ head broccoli, broken into florets
2 nests egg noodles or 120g (4¼oz)
   bronze-cut spaghetti
2 tbsp neutral oil
4 garlic cloves, grated
3 spring onions (scallions),
   finely sliced

For the sauce
2 tbsp light soy sauce
1 tbsp oyster sauce
½ tbsp dark soy sauce
½ tbsp toasted sesame oil
2 tbsp Sichuan chilli oil or Lao Gan
   Ma Crispy Chilli Oil
½ tbsp golden caster (superfine)
   sugar

Broccoli is probably my most consumed vegetable. I love it. I love all kinds, cooked in all ways. I always try to find a way to incorporate it into any dish. Luckily, it fits into this one perfectly.

Beef and broccoli are commonly cooked like this in China, as a stir fry, and served with rice. This recipe is inspired by the dish Gai Lan Chao Niu Rou, which features beef and gai lan (Chinese broccoli), but uses English broccoli instead, a combination that is often seen in Chinese restaurants in the UK nowadays, reflecting the availability of ingredients from region to region. I've incorporated this combination with noodles here (instead of the more traditional stir fry plus rice).

1   In a bowl, mix together the cornflour (cornstarch), 1 tbsp water and the light soy. Marinate the steak in this mixture, coating well, while you prep the rest of the ingredients.

2   Bring a large pan of water to the boil. Add the broccoli florets and cook for 3–5 minutes until just softened but still green. Scoop out directly into a bowl of ice-cold water. Set aside.

3   In the same pan, cook the noodles for 2 minutes less than what is stated on the packet instructions. We want them to remain al dente. Strain and rinse under cool water, separating the noodles with your fingers, to prevent them from sticking. Set aside.

4   Mix all the sauce ingredients and set aside.

5   Then, heat 1 tbsp of the neutral oil in a wok or non-stick, heavy-based frying pan (skillet). Add the steak and cook for 3–5 minutes until browned and caramelized. Remove the steak from the pan and wipe the pan.

6   Add the remaining 1 tbsp neutral oil to the clean pan and set over a medium-high heat. Add the garlic and stir fry for 30 seconds. Add the blanched broccoli and the steak. Toss and cook for 1 minute.

7   Give the noodles another quick rinse in cool water to make sure they're not stuck together. Add them to the pan and toss with the veg and beef. Add the sauce, toss to combine, then add the spring onions (scallions), toss and let wilt for 30 seconds.

8   Remove the pan from the heat and serve.

Weeknight Pad Thai

SERVES 2

240g (8½oz) flat, wide rice
   (pad Thai) noodles
5 tbsp tamarind concentrate
3 tbsp palm sugar or light (soft)
   brown sugar
3 tbsp fish sauce
1–2 tbsp neutral oil
2 eggs
80g (3oz) firm pressed tofu, diced
2 large garlic cloves, grated
   or crushed
12 frozen king prawns (jumbo
   shrimp), defrosted
2 handfuls of bean sprouts
2 spring onions (scallions),
   chopped into 2.5cm (1in) pieces
2 tbsp salted peanuts,
   roughly chopped
2 limes, wedged
1 tbsp Sichuan chilli (red pepper)
   flakes or gochugaru

There is a lot to say and a lot to know about Pad Thai. It's a dish that appears simple, but is complex and difficult to perfect.

One of the most memorable Pad Thai I have ever eaten was in Bangkok's Chinatown. It was unforgettable, not only because the noodles were delicious, and served inside a little parcel with wrapping made from an intricate lacy omelette, but also because the chef was expertly handling his wok over a roaring flame, blaring rock music, while wearing a cowboy hat and a T-shirt with Snoopy on it.

There are a lot of recipes out there for Pad Thai. It's a dish that I enjoy cooking and eating at home. This simplified version is an easy, lazy adaptation for weeknights and tired heads. Food writer Leela Punyaratabandhu has a great Pad Thai guide on her blog, *She Simmers*. I can't get the fresh rice Pad Thai noodles she suggests, but do try them if you can. Preserved radishes are traditionally used but I also find them hard to come by. I use spring onions (scallions) instead of Chinese chives, as they are more readily available.

1   Soak the noodles in boiling water according to the packet instructions or until al dente. It's important not to overcook the noodles, or they will break apart and clump together. Drain and rinse under cool water, separating the noodles with your fingers, to prevent them from sticking.

2   Combine the tamarind concentrate, sugar and fish sauce in a bowl or jug (pitcher), until the sugar is dissolved, to make the sauce. Set aside.

3   Heat 1 tbsp of oil in a large non-stick, heavy-based frying pan (skillet) or wok over a high heat. Fry the eggs on both sides until just set. Using the edge of a spatula, break the eggs up into 4 or 5 pieces and move them to the side of the pan. Add a little more oil if needed. Add the tofu and garlic and stir fry for 2 minutes, until the tofu begins to turn golden.

4   Add the prawns and stir fry everything together quickly, ensuring that the pan remains over the highest heat. Once the prawns begin to turn pink, add the bean sprouts and spring onions (scallions) and stir fry for 30 seconds. Add the noodles, quickly followed by the sauce, and toss everything together. Work quickly – you don't want the noodles to be in the pan for too long, or they will clump and break up. Once the sauce is just warmed through, remove from the heat and serve.

5   Garnish with peanuts, lime wedges and Sichuan chilli (red pepper) flakes.

Salt and Pepper Squid Noodles

SERVES 2

2 nests fresh or dried lo mein thick
    egg noodles
2 tbsp light soy sauce
2 tsp maple syrup
1 tsp white rice vinegar
2 tsp toasted sesame oil
1 tbsp sriracha
2 tbsp neutral oil
1 medium onion, sliced
2.5cm (1in) ginger, peeled
    and grated
4 large garlic cloves, crushed
    or grated
3 spring onions (scallions),
    finely shredded
250g (9oz) frozen squid rings
    or tubes, defrosted and sliced
    into rings
1 small red (bell) pepper,
    finely shredded
1 red chilli, sliced
1 green chilli, sliced
1 tbsp salt and pepper seasoning
1 lime, wedged
1 small handful of coriander
    (cilantro), roughly chopped

Salt and pepper squid (S&P Squid) is one of my all-time favourite things to eat. It's not just that I love squid – and I do, I really do – it's the serious amount of 'gubbins' (aka delicious bits) in this that I can't get enough of. Not to mention the chillies, onion and garlic, intermingled with the crispy batter of the squid, all sat atop some fresh crunchy lettuce, as it is often at some of my favourite restaurants. It's poetic!

This is reminiscent of the flavours of S&P squid, and all those addictive gubbins, but is stir-fried and served here with noodles. The success of this recipe is dictated by the salt and pepper seasoning mix – which is perfectly balanced and will give the dish that moreish flavour. You can find it online or at East and Southeast Asian supermarkets. My favourite brand is KMC.

1   Bring a pan of water to the boil and cook the noodles for 1 minute less than what is stated on the packet instructions. Drain and rinse under cool water, separating the noodles with your fingers, to prevent them from sticking. Set aside.

2   Meanwhile, combine the light soy, maple syrup, vinegar, sesame oil and sriracha in a jug (pitcher) to make the sauce. Set aside.

3   Heat the neutral oil in a non-stick, heavy-based frying pan (skillet) or wok and add the onion. Stir fry for 2–3 minutes, until it begins to turn translucent. Add the ginger, garlic and spring onions (scallions) and stir fry for 1 minute, keeping everything moving to prevent burning. Add the defrosted squid and stir fry for 1 minute. Add the (bell) pepper and chillies. Stir fry for 1 minute. Add the salt and pepper seasoning and distribute well over the squid and the aromatics.

4   Add the noodles and the sauce and toss to coat. Serve with the lime wedges and coriander (cilantro).

Full English Yakisoba

SERVES 2

2 nests fresh or dried yakisoba
  noodles
3 tsp toasted sesame oil
1 tsp dashi powder
2 tbsp light soy sauce
3 tbsp Japanese Worcestershire
  sauce
1 tbsp oyster sauce
2 tbsp mirin
¼ tsp sea salt
¼ tsp freshly ground black pepper
3 tsp neutral oil
3 smoked streaky bacon rashers,
  chopped into 2cm (5in) pieces
  (or use unsmoked, if you prefer)
8 chestnut (cremini) mushrooms,
  quartered
½ onion, sliced
2 spring onions (scallions),
  chopped into 2.5cm (1in) pieces
2 eggs
1 tbsp furikake

A full English has to be one of my most-eaten meals. As a kid, often the only things left in the fridge and cupboards were those for a fry up; things that don't go off so quickly: canned baked beans, bacon, eggs. Even into adulthood, I will often have a fry-up for dinner, or 'brinner' (breakfast for dinner) as I've heard it referred to. Of course, the more traditional carb would be toast, or a hash brown, or both. But I'm also partial to a fry-up with a noodle, especially when it's for brinner.

I skip red and brown sauce on my fry-ups – I don't think they need it. But, a large percentage of Brits do serve theirs with brown sauce. The flavours of brown sauce are not dissimilar to the sweeter Japanese Worcestershire sauce – especially the fruitier varieties – and this led me to the conclusion that a Yakisoba-style noodle dish, which is usually tossed with the thick sauce, is a great match. And, trust me, it works, really, really well.

1   Cook the yakisoba noodles according to the packet instructions. Drain and rinse under cool water, separating the noodles with your fingers, to prevent them from sticking. Dress with 1 tsp of the toasted sesame oil and set aside.

2   Combine the remaining 2 tsp sesame oil, dashi powder, light soy, Worcestershire sauce, oyster sauce, mirin, salt and pepper in a jug (pitcher) to make the sauce. Set aside.

3   Heat 1 tsp of the neutral oil in a non-stick, heavy-based frying pan (skillet), over a medium-high heat, and add the bacon pieces. Without stirring, allow these to sit and crisp up while the fat renders. After 2–3 minutes, add the mushrooms and stir fry with the bacon. Add the onion and continue to stir fry for 1 minute. Add the spring onions (scallions), and stir fry for 30 seconds before adding the noodles, followed by the sauce. Stir fry everything for a further 1–2 minutes, until everything is incorporated well and the noodles have absorbed any remaining sauce. Remove from the heat.

4   In a clean non-stick pan, with the remaining 2 tsp neutral oil, fry the eggs to your liking.

5   Serve the noodles, topped with a fried egg and garnished with furikake.

Freezer-raid Spicy Seafood Udon

SERVES 4

6 tbsp light soy sauce

2 tbsp oyster sauce

2 tbsp gochugaru

4 tbsp gochujang

2 tbsp mirin

½ tbsp dashi powder

2 tbsp maple syrup

1 tsp toasted sesame oil

1 tbsp neutral oil

2.5cm (1in) ginger, peeled and grated

5 large garlic cloves, crushed or grated

1 small carrot, peeled and finely shredded

1 green chilli, sliced

1 medium onion, thickly sliced

4 nests frozen udon noodles

16 frozen king prawns (jumbo shrimp), defrosted

2 frozen large, cleaned squid, tentacles included, defrosted and sliced into rings

8 fish balls, defrosted (I like fried prawn fish balls or lobster balls, but you can use any)

4 handfuls of frozen clams

1 small courgette (zucchini), finely shredded

6 spring onions (scallions), chopped into 5cm (2in) pieces

Seafood is one of my favourite things to have stashed away in the freezer. East and Southeast Asian supermarkets and wholesalers have such a vast range of high-quality produce. I will usually keep scored squid, peeled king prawns (jumbo shrimp), whole tiger prawns (shell on), whole squid, cleaned clams and prepared unagi (freshwater eel).

Another favourite thing to keep stashed in the freezer is udon noodles. Udon noodles are so thick that they don't really work too well dried, and I prefer the finished texture of the frozen ones, which retain their texture really well and are nice and al dente but still soft and slippery when cooked. The crème de la crème is ordering them fresh, if I want to treat myself.

These noodles are heavily inspired by the delicious flavours of Jjamppong – a Chinese-style Korean seafood noodle soup that utilizes gochujang and dried anchovies to create a spicy bowl of seafood goodness. These noodles are brothless, but I incorporate the flavour of the anchovy dashi into the noodles using bonito stock granules (a super useful ingredient for making quick-sharp dashi stock).

1   Combine the light soy, oyster sauce, gochugaru, gochujang, mirin, dashi, maple syrup and sesame oil in a jug to make the sauce. Set aside.

2   Bring a large saucepan of water to the boil, ready to cook the noodles.

3   In a large non-stick, heavy-based frying pan (skillet) or wok, heat the neutral oil over a high heat. Add the ginger and garlic and stir fry for 30 seconds until fragrant. Add the carrots, chilli and onion, and continue to stir fry for 1–2 minutes.

4   Drop the noodles into the boiling water and move them around slightly to avoid them sticking to the bottom of the pan. Set a timer for the amount of time stated on the packet.

→

5   Meanwhile, push the carrots and onion to one side of the pan. Add the prawns (shrimp) and squid and cook for 2–3 minutes, keeping everything moving to ensure the pan stays hot and nothing burns. Add the fish balls, frozen clams and courgette (zucchini). Continue to stir fry everything for 1 minute to bring the pan back up to temperature.

6   Add the sauce, along with a splash of the noodle cooking water. Let the sauce bubble away gently for 2–3 minutes or until the clams begin to open. If any clams remain closed, remove them. Add the chopped spring onions (scallions).

7   When the timer for the noodles goes off, add the noodles straight from their pan, using tongs, into the seafood mix. Let the pan simmer for 1–2 minutes or until the sauce has thickened. Toss to coat and serve.

Black Bean Mushroom Noodles

SERVES 2 · VG

60g (2¼oz) dried mixed
   mushrooms
2 tbsp neutral oil
6 large garlic cloves, crushed
1 onion, diced
1 small carrot, diced
1 green chilli, diced
2 dried red Chinese chillies
200g (7oz) chestnut (cremini)
   mushrooms, roughly chopped
100g (3½oz) fresh shiitake, roughly
   chopped stalks removed
½ tsp sea salt
3 tbsp Korean black bean paste
   (chunjang)
2 tbsp vegetarian oyster sauce
1 tbsp hoisin sauce
2 nests Taiwanese flower petal
   noodles
½ cucumber, deseeded and
   shredded
2 spring onions (scallions),
   shredded

This dish is a vegetarian riff on the Korean dish Jajangmyeon (page 138). However, it really does stand alone as a recipe in its own right, as opposed to a vegetarian alternative – especially if, like me, you love mushrooms.

If you can't find fresh shiitake, use whatever mushrooms you like. For delicate mushrooms like oyster, simply tear them. King oyster mushrooms should be sliced and scored with a cross hatch, as they can be tough to chew. Enoki and shimeji can be kept whole. Delicate mushrooms like these will need less cooking and can be added to the sauce 5 minutes before the end.

1   Soak the dried mixed mushrooms in a mug of boiling water for 10–15 minutes, until softened. Strain and reserve the soaking liquor.

2   Heat the neutral oil in a non-stick, heavy-based frying pan (skillet) over a medium-high heat. Add the garlic, onion and carrot. Stir fry for 1–2 minutes, until the onion just begins to turn translucent. Add the fresh and dried chillies, and continue to stir fry. Add the fresh and rehydrated mushrooms with the salt and stir fry for 1–2 minutes. Once the mushrooms have begun to brown, turn down the heat and let them sit, not stirring, for 4–5 minutes, ensuring the mushrooms are well spread out so that any moisture can evaporate and the mushrooms don't boil.

3   Add the Korean black bean paste, vegetarian oyster sauce and hoisin sauce, along with the mushroom soaking liquor. Stir to combine and let simmer for 5 minutes.

4   Meanwhile, cook the noodles according to the packet instructions.

5   Serve the noodles hot, topped with the mushroom sauce, shredded cucumber and spring onions (scallions).

Duck Vermicelli

SERVES 2

2 nests dried rice vermicelli
   noodles
½ tbsp toasted sesame oil
2 tbsp light soy sauce
1 tbsp kecap manis
¼ tsp freshly ground black pepper
½ tsp light (soft) brown sugar
1 tsp dark soy sauce
1 tbsp neutral oil
2 garlic cloves, grated or crushed
1 small carrot, finely shredded
1 long red chilli, sliced
2 pak choi (bok choy), stems
   removed and leaves separated
250g (9oz) shredded takeaway
   duck meat, or 1 frozen bone-in
   aromatic crispy duck half (around
   400–500g/14–18oz will yield
   the correct amount of meat)
   prepared according to packet
   instructions, meat shredded
2 handfuls of bean sprouts
3 spring onions (scallions),
   chopped into 2.5cm (1in) pieces

For me, duck is such a treat. The only times I ever remember eating it as a child were at Chinese restaurants, and I absolutely loved it. Whether it was in crispy duck pancakes, or roasted Hong Kong style, the flavour and texture is unbeatable.

Crispy duck is difficult to get right at home and so to keep things simple for this recipe I suggest using a pre-prepared crispy duck from an East and Southeast Asian supermarket, or from your local Chinese takeaway.

1. Cook the vermicelli noodles for 1–2 minutes less than stated on the packet instructions. We want these to be al dente, as they will continue cooking in the pan. If they're overcooked, they will break up into small strands. Once al dente, strain and rinse under cool water, separating the noodles with your fingers, to prevent them from sticking. Toss in the sesame oil and set aside.

2. Combine the light soy, kecap manis, black pepper, sugar and dark soy in a jug (pitcher) to make the sauce. Set aside.

3. Heat the neutral oil in a non-stick, heavy-based frying pan (skillet) or wok over a high heat. Add the garlic and stir fry for 30 seconds until fragrant. Add the carrot, chilli and pak choi (bok choy) and stir fry quickly for a further 2 minutes until the pak choi begins to wilt. Add the duck and stir fry for a further minute.

4. Add the bean sprouts and spring onions (scallions) and cook for a further minute, before adding the softened vermicelli noodles. Allow the ingredients to sit for 30 seconds, to catch a little char on the noodles and spring onions (scallions), before tossing again.

5. Add the sauce and mix well to incorporate. Keep on the heat for 1–2 minutes, until the sauce is just heated through – any longer and the noodles may become overcooked. Serve immediately.

Sticky BBQ Chicken Noodles

SERVES 4

For the chicken
2 tbsp light soy sauce
1 tbsp mirin
1 tsp cornflour (cornstarch)
4 boneless chicken thighs,
   chopped into chunks

For the noodles
4 nests fresh or dried thick
   wheat noodles
2 tbsp neutral oil
2 tsp Shaoxing rice wine
4 large garlic cloves, grated
   or crushed
1 courgette (zucchini), chopped
   into batons
2 spring onions (scallions),
   finely shredded
1 tbsp toasted sesame seeds

For the sauce
2 tbsp light soy sauce
1 tbsp mirin
2 tbsp apple cider vinegar
2 tbsp gochujang
4 tbsp shacha sauce
2 tbsp maple syrup
1 tbsp toasted sesame oil
1 tsp chicken bouillon powder
½ tsp sea salt

This recipe is perfect for when you're after something sweet, sticky and spicy. Shacha sauce makes a huge difference here – it's a Taiwanese condiment, made from garlic, shallots, shrimp and chillies. It's sometimes referred to as BBQ sauce and is typically used to make dips or marinades. It's incredibly savoury and moreish and a quick way to inject a lot of flavour into a dish with minimal hassle.

Use a good non-stick pan for this recipe, as the mirin and maple syrup will cause the lovely sticky sauce to caramelize and stick to the pan, which can cause it to burn quickly.

1   Combine the light soy sauce, mirin and cornflour (cornstarch) in a bowl to form a slurry. Add the chicken pieces and leave to marinate while you prepare the rest of the ingredients.

2   Cook the noodles according to the packet instructions. Drain and rinse under cool water, separating the noodles with your fingers, to prevent them from sticking. Set aside.

3   To make the sauce, combine all the ingredients in a jug (pitcher) and mix well. Set aside.

4   Heat the neutral oil in a non-stick, heavy-based frying pan (skillet) or wok, over a high heat. Add the chicken pieces and, without stirring, fry in the oil until they begin to crisp. Turn to brown on all sides. As the marinade begins to stick, add the Shaoxing rice wine to deglaze the pan. This should take around 3–4 minutes. Once browned, add the garlic and courgette (zucchini) and stir fry with the chicken. Add the sauce and let this bubble away for 1–2 minutes.

5   Add the noodles, toss to combine and remove from the heat. Serve topped with the spring onions (scallions) and sesame seeds.

Pad See Ew

SERVES 2

240g (8½oz) fresh or dried wide
    rice noodles
2 tbsp Thai thin soy sauce
1 tsp Thai black soy sauce
2 tbsp Thai oyster sauce
1 tbsp golden caster (superfine)
    sugar
¼ tsp freshly ground black pepper
1 tbsp Bull Head Shallot Sauce
2–3 tbsp neutral oil
2 eggs
250g (9oz) boneless pork loin or
    skinless boneless chicken thigh,
    chopped into bitesize pieces
4 large garlic cloves, crushed
    or grated
1 tbsp fish sauce
1 handful of kai lan or long-
    stemmed broccoli, chopped
    into 2.5cm (1in) pieces – if the
    stems are thick, halve them, so
    they have a diameter less than
    1cm (½in).

Thai Pad See Ew, which translates as 'stir-fried noodles' relies on the phenomenon that is wok hei, aka 'wok's breath' – the char and crunch that comes from cooking with a wok over a searing hot flame (page 21). Using a thin, carbon steel wok over the highest heat possible is essential. Do not overcrowd the pan, or the noodles will turn to gum – cook in batches if you need to. When adding ingredients to a pan, the temperature drops dramatically. Heat is important here. Ensure there is space between the ingredients, as you add them, and keep them moving.

Fresh rice noodles are best for this, but if you can't find them, use the widest dried rice noodle you can get.

1   Cook the noodles according to the packet instructions. If they're fresh, they will simply need dunking into some hot water and separating. Set aside.

2   Combine the thin soy, black soy, oyster sauce, sugar, pepper and shallot sauce in a jug (pitcher) to make the sauce. Set aside.

3   Heat the neutral oil in a wok, over the highest heat possible. Fry the eggs on both sides until just set. Using the edge of a spatula, break the eggs up into 4 or 5 pieces and move them to the side of the pan.

4   Add a little more oil, if needed, then add the pork (or chicken) and stir fry quickly for 30 seconds. Add the garlic and stir fry for another 30 seconds. Add the fish sauce and stir everything together, including the eggs. Add the kai lan (or long-stemmed broccoli), and keep everything moving for a further 2–3 minutes, until the broccoli begins to soften but remains bright green.

5   Add the softened noodles and toss them through the ingredients in the wok. Spread them out well and allow them to sit in contact with the wok, without stirring, for 30 seconds or so, to catch some char. The edges should blacken very slightly and a smoky smell should arise. Toss the noodles and repeat this step.

6   Add the sauce and toss to coat the noodles. Cook for a further minute and serve.

Beef and Black Bean Noodles

SERVES 4

2 tbsp fermented black beans

2 tbsp light soy sauce

1 tsp dark soy sauce

¼ tsp freshly ground black pepper

1 tbsp Shaoxing rice wine

1 tsp cornflour (cornstarch)

2 ribeye or sirloin steaks,
   thinly sliced

2.5cm (1in) ginger, peeled and
   grated, juice reserved

2 large garlic cloves, grated

4 nests medium egg noodles
   or lo mein thick egg noodles

1 tbsp neutral oil

1 small onion, sliced

1 green (bell) pepper,
   finely shredded

1–2 large green chillies, sliced

200ml (7fl oz) low-salt/salt-free
   chicken or beef stock

1 tsp light (soft) brown sugar

3 spring onions (scallions), finely
   shredded or sliced

Beef in black bean sauce is a typical Chinese restaurant dish and utilizes fermented black beans. The fermentation process creates a deeply savoury and umami flavour that is used widely in cuisines around the world but is very well known for its place in Chinese cookery, especially in popular Cantonese dishes such as spare ribs with black beans. This recipe pairs my ode to the classic combination with noodles.

1   Place the black beans in a bowl and cover with 100ml (3½oz) boiling water. Let them sit for 10–15 minutes while you prepare the rest of the ingredients.

2   Add the light soy, dark soy, black pepper, Shaoxing rice wine and cornflour (cornstarch) to a small bowl. Mix well to form a slurry. Add the sliced steak and mix to coat. Set aside.

3   Once the black beans are soaked, strain well and pat dry with paper towel. Return to the bowl and mash with the back of a fork. Mix with the grated ginger and reserved juice and the garlic.

4   Cook the noodles according to the packet instructions. Drain and rinse under cool water, separating the noodles with your fingers, to prevent them from sticking.

5   Heat the neutral oil in a non-stick, heavy-based frying pan (skillet) or wok over a medium-high heat. Using tongs, transfer the beef from the marinade into the pan, allowing any excess marinade to drip back into the bowl – don't discard the marinade. Fry the beef, spreading it out in the pan to allow the air to circulate. Let the beef sit and become browned and crispy. Then, stir fry on all sides for 2–3 minutes.

6   Add the onion, (bell) pepper and green chilli and continue to stir fry for 1–2 minutes. Move the beef and vegetables to the side of the pan and add the black bean paste. Fry this off for a minute until it becomes fragrant. Add the remaining beef marinade, along with the stock and sugar and stir well to combine. Allow this to simmer until thickened slightly.

7   Add the noodles and toss to coat. Cook for 1–2 minutes or until the noodles have soaked up any excess sauce, are coated and glossy. Serve immediately garnished with the spring onions (scallions).

My Favourite Cabbage Noodles

SERVES 2

4 dried shiitake mushrooms

2–3 nests mung bean vermicelli noodles

1 tbsp light soy sauce

1 tsp dark soy sauce

1 tbsp oyster sauce

¼ tsp sea salt

1 tsp golden caster (superfine) sugar

½ tsp chicken bouillon powder or mushroom bouillon powder

2 tbsp neutral oil

2 eggs, beaten

2 garlic cloves, grated

½ small Taiwanese, sweetheart (hispi) or green cabbage, shredded

½ carrot, finely shredded

My cravings for different flavours vary depending on my mood, but one thing that does not vary is my craving for texture – I always want crunch. So, for me, cabbage is an unsung hero. Chinese stir-fried cabbage, especially, has to be one of my most desired vegetable dishes. Known as Shou Si Bao Cai, which translates as 'hand-torn cabbage', it's a simple dish that, again, is most special with wok hei (see page 21). The cabbage is lightly charred, but still incredibly crisp and crunchy with just the right amount of give. This recipe is inspired by that dish. This is my love letter to cabbage.

1   Soak the shiitake mushrooms in a mug of boiling water for 10 minutes, while you prepare the rest of the ingredients. Once softened, remove and discard the stems and slice thinly. Set aside.

2   Soften the noodles according to the packet instructions.

3   Meanwhile, to make the sauce, mix the light soy, dark soy, oyster sauce, salt, sugar, and bouillon powder in a jug (pitcher) until the sugar and bouillon have dissolved. Set aside.

4   Heat 1 tbsp of the neutral oil in a non-stick, heavy-based frying pan (skillet) or wok over a medium-high heat. Add the eggs and scramble until cooked through. Remove from the pan and set aside.

5   Wipe the pan, return to the heat and add the remaining 1 tbsp oil. Add the garlic and fry for 30 seconds until fragrant. Add the cabbage, shiitake and carrot and stir fry quickly until the cabbage has wilted. Allow it to keep contact with the pan for 1–2 minutes, so the edges char slightly. Add the softened noodles, scrambled eggs and the sauce and stir fry to combine everything well. Serve immediately.

Black Bean Tofu Noodles

SERVES 4 · V

2 tbsp fermented black beans
2 tbsp light soy sauce
¼ tsp freshly ground black pepper
2 tsp toasted sesame oil
1 tsp dark soy sauce
1 tsp light (soft) brown sugar
2.5cm (1in) ginger, peeled and
   grated, juice reserved
2 large garlic cloves, grated
4 nests medium egg noodles
   or lo mein noodles
2 tbsp neutral oil
300g (10½oz) firm tofu or fried
   tofu, sliced into 1cm (½in) pieces
1 large green chilli, sliced
1 small onion, sliced
1 green (bell) pepper,
   finely shredded
200ml (7fl oz) vegetable stock
1 tsp cornflour (cornstarch)
4 spring onions (scallions),
   chopped into 2.5cm (1in) pieces,
   plus 1 sliced, to serve

I miss the umami saltiness of fermented black beans when I haven't dined out at a Chinese restaurant for a while. There's something so uniquely moreish about their flavour. Before I knew how to cook with them at home, I felt daunted by their preparation; however, they are simple to cook with and they keep for ages in the cupboard. When I feel the urge coming on (and if I'm not planning to eat out), I'll pop some black beans in a mug and cover them in boiling water – usually this will be adjacent to a cup of tea in the making – and leave them to soak until it's time to cook.

1   Place the black beans in a bowl and cover with 100ml (3½oz) boiling water. Let them sit for 10–15 minutes while you prepare the rest of the ingredients.

2   Combine the light soy sauce, black pepper, sesame oil, dark soy and sugar in a jug (pitcher) to make the sauce. Set aside.

3   Once the black beans are soaked, strain well and pat dry with paper towel. Add to a bowl and mash with the back of a fork. Mix with the grated ginger and reserved juice and the garlic.

4   Cook the noodles according to the packet instructions. Drain and rinse under cool water, separating the noodles with your fingers, to prevent them from sticking. Set aside.

5   Heat the neutral oil in a non-stick, heavy-based frying pan (skillet) or wok over a medium-high heat. Fry the tofu slices for 2 minutes on either side, until golden brown. Remove from the pan and set aside.

6   Add the black bean paste to the pan and stir fry for 1 minute until fragrant. Add the green chilli, onion and green (bell) pepper and continue to stir fry for a further minute. Add the sauce, along with the stock and mix to combine. Bring this to a gentle simmer.

7   In a mug, mix the cornflour (cornstarch) with 1 tbsp cold water to form a slurry and set aside.

8   Add the tofu back to the black bean sauce, along with the chopped spring onions (scallions). Add the cornflour (cornstarch) slurry and mix well. Once the sauce has thickened slightly, add the noodles and toss everything together. Serve immediately and garnish with the sliced spring onions.

Creamy Miso Mushroom Udon

SERVES 2 · V

15g (½oz) dried and shredded black fungus mushrooms
4 dried or fresh shiitake mushrooms
2 nests fresh, dried or frozen udon noodles
1 tbsp white miso
1 tbsp cream cheese
1 tbsp light soy sauce
1 tsp light (soft) brown sugar
¼ tsp freshly ground black pepper
1 tbsp neutral oil
1 tbsp butter
2 garlic cloves, crushed or grated
1 portobello mushroom, finely sliced
150g (5½oz) shimeji mushrooms
¼ tsp sea salt
2 small handfuls of bean sprouts
2 spring onions (scallions), whites and greens chopped into 2cm (1in) pieces, plus some greens finely sliced to serve

Cream cheese is another ingredient that, when I have it in the fridge, I feel like the possibilities are endless. This combination might not strike you as one you might use to dress noodles, but it's an easy way to add flavour and body to a sauce with minimal fuss and ingredients. The addition of soy sauce and miso paste adds an umami, salty depth. It's the kind of recipe that once you've made it once, you'll no longer need the recipe at all – it's that simple.

1   Rehydrate the black fungus and shiitake mushrooms (if using dried) in a mug of hot water for 10–15 minutes. Strain, reserving the soaking liquor.

2   Meanwhile, cook the noodles according to the packet instructions. Drain and rinse under cool water, separating the noodles with your fingers, to prevent them from sticking.

3   Combine the miso, cream cheese, light soy sauce, sugar, black pepper and mushroom soaking liquor in a jug to make the sauce. Set aside.

4   Heat the neutral oil in a non-stick, heavy-based frying pan (skillet) or wok over a medium-high heat. Add the butter and garlic and stir fry for 30 seconds until fragrant. Add the sliced portobello mushrooms and fry on both sides until browned. Add the shiitake, black fungus and shimeji mushrooms, then the salt, and stir fry for 2–3 minutes.

5   Add the bean sprouts and chopped spring onion (scallion) pieces and stir fry for 1 minute. Add the noodles and stir fry for a further minute. Turn the heat to the lowest setting. Add the sauce and toss well to combine, heating very gently until just warmed through. Garnish with the sliced spring onions, remove from the heat and serve.

Winter Beef Curry Udon

SERVES 4

1 tbsp neutral oil

350g–400g (14oz) bavette (flank) steak, sliced

2 large garlic cloves, crushed or grated

1 small onion, thickly sliced

2 small or 1 medium carrot, finely sliced (see note)

90g (3¼oz) Japanese curry block (I like Java Curry), roughly chopped

200g (7oz) cavolo nero or kale, chopped into 2.5cm (1in) pieces, tough stalks removed

¼ tsp sea salt

1 large handful of frozen peas

4 nests fresh or frozen udon noodles

4 tbsp pickled ginger

NOTE
For neat, thinly sliced carrots, use a mandoline (carefully!).

Japanese curry blocks, or curry roux, are an indispensable store-cupboard staple. They don't last long in my house, so I tend to stock up. They're an easy way to create a quick and tasty meal, using just the block and water – and then customizing depending on the ingredients you have to hand.

I like Golden Mountain brand, medium hot, but my new all-time favourite – a recommendation from my trusty friend, restaurateur and cook Tim Anderson – is Java Curry.

Katsu (breadcrumbed and fried pork or chicken, served with curry) is one of the most popular ways to eat this kind of curry, but it's also commonly served with slow-braised beef and potatoes, on top of rice. In Japanese curry chains, you can choose toppings such as scrambled egg or tempura prawn and customize with corn, kimchi or other tasty things.

I can eat Japanese curry come rain or shine, but the winter months draw me to thick udon noodles with wholesome vegetables.

1   Heat the neutral oil in a non-stick, heavy-based frying pan (skillet) over a high heat. Fry the bavette (flank) slices for 2–3 minutes on either side until browned all over. Remove from the pan and set aside to rest.

2   In the same pan, fry the garlic for 30 seconds. Add the onion and carrot and stir fry quickly for 1–2 minutes. Add 800ml (28fl oz) water, followed by the curry block. Stir until the curry blocks dissolve, then reduce the heat.

3   Return the beef to the pan with the cavolo nero and salt and let the curry simmer for 10–15 minutes, until the carrots are softened. Throw in the frozen peas and cook for another minute.

4   Meanwhile, cook the noodles according to the packet instructions. Once ready, strain and divide into 4 deep bowls. Top with the curry and serve immediately, with a side of pickled ginger.

Tempura Soba

SERVES 2

8 frozen or chilled tempura prawns

2 nests dried soba noodles

100g (3½oz) choi sum or pak choi
   (bok choy), chopped into 2.5cm
   (1in) pieces

1 tbsp sake

2 tbsp mirin

2 tbsp Japanese soy sauce

1 tbsp dashi powder

1 spring onion (scallion),
   finely sliced

2 tsp toasted sesame oil

Simple, warming and delicious. This Japanese-style recipe requires little fresh produce – the greens can be swapped out for whatever you find lying in the bottom of your fridge, and if you don't have anything fresh in, just leave it out. It also saves time by using ready-made tempura prawns, so there's no need to make a batter or use another pan for frying. You can also buy ready-made dashi to make it even speedier – my favourite is from Koya restaurant in London. I would have an IV of that stuff if I could, it's so good.

1   Cook the tempura prawns according to the packet instructions. I find this quickest and simplest in the air fryer, but you can do it in the oven, too.

2   When there are 10 minutes left for the prawns, bring a pan of water to the boil and drop in the soba noodles and choi sum pieces. Cook for 4 minutes (or the time stated on the noodle packet). Drain the noodles and greens and rinse with cool water to stop them from sticking. Set aside.

3   Into each serving bowl, add ½ tbsp sake, 1 tbsp mirin and 1 tbsp Japanese soy sauce.

4   Dissolve the dashi powder in 500ml (17fl oz) boiling water. Pour 250ml (9fl oz) hot stock into each serving bowl and mix to combine with the seasonings. Divide the noodles and greens between the bowls and top with the prawn tempura and sliced spring onion (scallion). Drizzle with sesame oil and serve.

Aubergine Doubanjiang Noodles

SERVES 2 · VG

4 dried shiitake mushrooms

2 nests thick wheat noodles

1 tbsp neutral oil

2 garlic cloves, grated

1 large aubergine (eggplant),
  chopped into 1cm (½in) cubes

1½ tbsp doubanjiang

2 tbsp Chinkiang black rice vinegar

1 tsp dark soy sauce

1 tbsp light soy sauce

1 tsp toasted sesame oil

1 tbsp golden caster (superfine)
  sugar

Aubergines (eggplants) and doubanjiang are one of my all-time favourite combinations. This recipe is inspired by the Sichuan dish Yu Xiang, or 'fish-fragrant', named so not because it contains any fish but due to the heady, savoury flavour imparted by the doubanjiang, a spicy fermented bean sauce. Fish-fragrant aubergines (eggplants) also wouldn't typically be served with noodles (rather with rice or as a side), but this sauce works really well with wheat noodles.

1   Soak the mushrooms in a mug of boiling water for 15 minutes. Strain and slice the soaked mushrooms, and reserve the soaking liquor.

2   Meanwhile, cook the noodles according to the packet instructions. Drain and rinse under cool water, separating the noodles with your fingers, to prevent them from sticking. Set aside.

3   In a large non-stick, heavy-based frying pan (skillet), heat the oil over a medium-high heat. Add the garlic and stir fry for 30 seconds or until fragrant. Add the aubergine (eggplant) and the sliced mushrooms and stir fry for 2 minutes. Add the doubanjiang and stir well for 1–2 minutes or until it becomes fragrant. Add the vinegar, dark soy, light soy, sesame oil and sugar. Add the reserved mushroom soaking liquid, mix well and let it bubble away for 3–4 minutes or until the sauce thickens slightly. Add the noodles and stir to coat. Remove from the heat and serve immediately.

Chicken and Mushroom (Not) Noodles

SERVES 2

1 tbsp light soy sauce

1 tbsp oyster sauce

1 tsp dark soy sauce

1 tsp chicken bouillon powder

¼ tsp sea salt

1 tsp light (soft) brown sugar

1 tsp cornflour (cornstarch)

1 tbsp Shaoxing rice wine

2 boneless, skinless chicken thighs, chopped into cubes

2 nests Taiwanese flower petal noodles or ramen noodles

1 tbsp neutral oil

2 garlic cloves, grated or crushed

6 chestnut (cremini) mushrooms, quartered

4 tbsp sweetcorn

2 spring onions (scallions), finely diced

During my younger years, after nights out, me and my best friend would stumble back to his house and raid his kitchen cupboards for one thing: a pot (you know the one) of chicken and mushroom noodles. In our tipsy haze, while the noodles 'cooked', we'd make ourselves some toast, from white sliced bread, with proper butter. We would devour the lot, sat cross-legged in his single loft bed, before passing out fully dressed. The next morning we'd find the empty soy sauce sachet floating around the bed or, once, stuck to my cheek.

I don't think I've eaten a pot of such noodles since those years, but that's not to say I wouldn't. The flavour of this recipe is very much inspired by that little green pot.

1   Add the light soy sauce, oyster sauce, dark soy, chicken bouillon powder, salt, sugar, cornflour (cornstarch) and Shaoxing rice wine to a small bowl and stir to combine. Add the chicken pieces, toss to coat and let this sit for 10 minutes, while you cook the noodles according to the packet instructions.

2   Once the noodles are cooked, reserve about 200ml (7fl oz) of the cooking water, then strain and rinse the noodles under cool water, separating the noodles with your fingers, to prevent them from sticking. Set aside.

3   In a non-stick, heavy-based frying pan (skillet), heat the neutral oil over a medium-high heat. Add the garlic and stir fry until fragrant. Add the mushrooms and cook these for 3–4 minutes on all sides or until evenly browned. Add the chicken to the pan, along with the marinade, using a rubber spatula to scrape every last drop from the bowl. Add about 4 tbsp of the reserved noodle water, along with the sweetcorn. Stir to combine well and let the mixture gently simmer for 5–6 minutes. The sauce should be reduced and glossy.

4   Add the noodles and toss through the chicken and vegetables. Remove from the heat and top with the spring onions (scallions). Serve with or without white sliced toast.

Sweet and Savoury Stir-fried Noodles

SERVES 2

2 nests medium egg noodles
1 tsp toasted sesame oil
1 tbsp light soy sauce
1 tbsp kecap manis
1 tbsp sambal oelek, plus extra
    to serve
1 tsp dark soy sauce
1 tsp light (soft) brown sugar
1 tsp chicken bouillon powder
3 tbsp neutral oil
3 garlic cloves, grated or crushed
1 small shallot, or half a large
    shallot, sliced
12 large frozen king prawns (jumbo
    shrimp), defrosted
1 carrot, finely shredded
½ head Chinese leaf (napa
    cabbage) leaves, finely shredded
1 small handful of bean sprouts
2 eggs

Mie (Mee or Mi) Goreng is a delicious, stir-fried noodle dish from Indonesia, flavoured with super-savoury aromatics, such as shallots and garlic, with kecap manis – a sweet and sticky soy sauce. The Indonesian instant noodle brand Indomie has a Mi Goreng flavour and it's hailed as one of the best instant noodle packets you can buy, with more than 15 billion packets produced annually, sold in over 100 countries. I have consumed a lot of Indomie Mi Goreng in my time and this recipe is my ode to that beloved packet.

1   Cook the noodles according to the packet instructions. Drain and rinse under cool water, separating the noodles with your fingers, to prevent them from sticking. Add the sesame oil and toss to coat. Set aside.

2   Meanwhile, combine the light soy, kecap manis, sambal oelek, dark soy, sugar, chicken bouillon powder and 4 tbsp water in a jug (pitcher) to make the sauce. Stir well to dissolve and set aside.

3   Heat 2 tbsp of the neutral oil in a non-stick, heavy-based frying pan (skillet) or wok over a medium heat. When hot, add the garlic and stir fry for 30 seconds until fragrant. Add the shallot and cook for another 30 seconds, before adding the prawns (jumbo shrimp). Keep everything moving until the prawns turn pink on all sides. Add the carrot and continue to stir fry for 2–3 minutes. Add the Chinese leaf (napa cabbage) and stir fry for another minute.

4   Add the sauce and allow this to gently simmer for 2 minutes until the sauce is slightly thickened. Add the noodles and toss to coat. Add the bean sprouts and let these cook through in the noodles and sauce for 1 minute before removing from the heat.

5   In another frying pan (skillet) heat the remaining 1 tbsp neutral oil. When hot, fry the eggs until the yolk is runny and the edges are crisp, or however you like them.

6   Serve the noodles, topped with a fried egg. Add a dollop of sambal oelek on the side, if you'd like an extra kick.

Flat-pack Meatball Noodles

SERVES 2

12 store-bought meatballs
    (I use Swedish ones)
1 tbsp neutral oil
2.5cm (1in) ginger, peeled and
    finely shredded
2 garlic cloves, grated or crushed
½ Chinese leaf (napa cabbage),
    chopped into 2.5cm (1in) pieces
2 tbsp light soy sauce
1 tsp dark soy sauce
2 tbsp oyster sauce
1 tsp light (soft) brown sugar
4 tbsp chicken stock
1 tsp cornflour (cornstarch)
2 nests thin wheat noodles
2 spring onions (scallions),
    chopped into 2.5cm (1in) pieces

I have very fond memories of my gran taking me to a certain big, blue furniture store when I was a child, and we would always have the meatballs in the canteen. Now I take my children. It's such a treat and I enjoy them as much now as I did when I was a child. By the checkouts, you can buy them in bags, frozen, so I always have a stash of them at home. Normally, I will serve them with mash and peas, as they do; but, sometimes, if my freezer stash is a little depleted, I will use these meatballs on just about anything. It would be impossible for them to make a dish worse. The first time I used them to jazz up instant noodles was a revelation.

1   Cook the meatballs according to the packet instructions (I do these in the air fryer for speed).

2   Heat the neutral oil in a non-stick, heavy-based frying pan (skillet) over a medium heat. Add the ginger and garlic and stir fry for 30 seconds until fragrant. Add the cabbage and stir fry for 2 minutes or until just softened. Add the light soy, dark soy, oyster sauce, sugar and chicken stock and mix well until the sugar dissolves. Allow this to bubble for 2–3 minutes before adding the cooked meatballs and any fat that has collected in their baking tin.

3   Mix the cornflour (cornstarch) with 1 tbsp water to form a slurry. Stir into the sauce and let it bubble for 1–2 minutes or until thickened.

4   Meanwhile, cook the noodles according to the packet instructions.

5   Divide the noodles between two bowls and top with the meatballs and sauce. Garnish with the sliced spring onions (scallions).

Jajangmyeon

SERVES 2

2 tbsp neutral oil

200g (7oz) pork belly, chopped into 1cm (½in) cubes

1 medium onion, chopped into 1cm (½in) cubes

1 medium potato, peeled and chopped into 1cm (½in) cubes

1 tbsp golden caster (superfine) sugar

5 tbsp Korean black bean paste (chunjang)

1 tbsp oyster sauce

250ml (9fl oz) chicken stock, hot

1 small courgette (zucchini), chopped into 1cm (½in) cubes

½ small sweetheart (hispi) cabbage, chopped into 1cm (½in) cubes

2 nests fresh or dried thick wheat noodles (see note)

1 tbsp cornflour (cornstarch)

1 tsp toasted sesame oil

¼ cucumber, seeds removed and julienned

NOTE

If you can get hold of fresh wheat noodles for this dish, I would highly recommend it.

Jajangmyeon is a Korean noodle dish of pork and veggies in a thick, dark, bean sauce, usually topped with some crunchy fresh cucumber or spring onion (scallion). The combination of the deep, umami sauce and the fresh crunchy vegetables is mega moreish and quick to bring together.

Jajangmyeon originates from the Chinese dish Zhajiangmian; however, the dishes are very different, with different ingredients, preparations and flavours. There are many variations of Jajangmyeon, such as Euni Jajangmyeon, which is made with ground meat instead of diced, or Samseon Jajangmyeon, which is made with seafood instead of pork.

Traditionally, the dish relies upon chunjang, a Korean fermented black bean paste. You can find this online or in East and Southeast Asian supermarkets. If you can't get hold of chunjang, Chinese sweet bean paste (tian mian jiang) and a splash of dark soy sauce will give a similar look and flavour. Tian mian jiang is saltier and less umami, though, so be sure to adjust your seasoning accordingly.

1   Put a pan of water on to boil, ready to cook your noodles.

2   Heat the neutral oil in a non-stick, heavy-based frying pan (skillet) over a medium-high heat. Add the pork belly cubes and fry for 4–5 minutes, until they're beginning to brown on all sides. Add the onion and potato and continue to cook for another 3–4 minutes. Add the sugar and let this dissolve into the juices in the pan. After 1–2 minutes, it should begin to caramelize slightly. Add the Korean black bean paste and oyster sauce and mix well to coat the ingredients. Add the chicken stock and mix well. Reduce the heat and let this simmer for 4 minutes.

3   Add the courgette (zucchini) and cabbage to the sauce and continue to simmer for 6 minutes, or until the courgette has just softened but not lost its green colour.

4   Meanwhile, cook the noodles according to the packet instructions. Once cooked, strain and divide between two bowls.

5   Combine the cornflour (cornstarch) with 2 tbsp water to make a slurry. Add this to the pork and vegetables and stir. Cook for 2 minutes or until the sauce is thickened and dark, then remove from the heat. Stir through the sesame oil.

6   Serve the sauce over the noodles and top with the shredded cucumber.

Quick Spicy
Beef Noodle Broth

SERVES 4

3 tbsp beef fat or neutral oil

2.5cm (1in) ginger, peeled
and grated

3 large garlic cloves, grated
or crushed

4 spring onions (scallions), whites
and greens separated, finely sliced

1 medium onion, finely sliced

3 tbsp doubanjiang

1 large beef tomato, roughly
chopped

1.2L (42fl oz) beef bone broth
or stock

3 tbsp light soy sauce

2 tbsp light (soft) brown sugar

½ tsp freshly ground black pepper

2 bavette (flank) steaks

4 nests thick fresh wheat noodles

8 beef tendon balls or beef balls

2 heads pak choi (bok choy),
leaves separated, stem removed

1 handful of coriander (cilantro),
roughly chopped

When I found myself without the time or energy to make slow-cooked broths, I just stopped eating them at home altogether, unless they were instant. But I really began to miss them and started experimenting with ways to create a good and satisfying broth, quickly.

A top-quality base stock is needed but, fear not, these can be widely bought if you don't have time to make your own. During long slow braises, fat and connective tissue are broken down into the broth to give it body, texture and a meaty savoury flavour; however, there's no shortcut for slow-cooked meat. So, steak it is!

1   Heat 2 tbsp of the beef fat or oil in a large stock pot over a medium heat. Add the ginger and garlic and white parts of the spring onions (scallions) and stir fry for 30 seconds, until aromatic.

2   Add the onion and doubanjiang and stir fry for a further minute, before adding the tomato. Stir fry for 2 minutes until everything is well combined. Add the bone broth or stock, light soy sauce, sugar and black pepper. Mix well and let this simmer gently while you prepare the rest of the dish.

3   Heat the remaining 1 tbsp beef fat or oil in a non-stick, heavy-based frying pan (skillet) until very hot. Cook the bavette (flank) steaks for 3–4 minutes on both sides, until they are nicely browned all over. Remove from the pan and set aside to rest for at least 5 minutes.

4   Meanwhile, bring a pan of water to the boil, then add the noodles and beef balls. Cook according to the packet instructions. For the last minute of cooking time, drop in the pak choi (bok choy). Strain and divide the noodles, balls and pak choi between four bowls.

5   Check the broth for seasonings and adjust accordingly. Ladle the hot broth over the noodles. Slice the steak against the grain and serve on top of the noodles. Garnish with coriander (cilantro) and the sliced spring onion (scallion) greens.

Quick Soba Salad

SERVES 4

3 tbsp freshly squeezed lime juice

1 tbsp light soy sauce

1 tbsp maple syrup

2 tsp toasted sesame oil

¼ tsp sea salt

200g (7oz) long-stemmed
  broccoli

1 tsp neutral oil

1 small carrot, grated

¼ red cabbage, shredded

2 spring onions (scallions),
  finely sliced

1 small handful of coriander
  (cilantro), roughly chopped

1 small handful of mint,
  roughly chopped

4 nests dried soba noodles

1 ripe avocado, roughly chopped

1 tbsp furikake

1 handful of shelled pistachios,
  roughly chopped

I love to serve this salad at our biannual family gathering, where it's devoured by 50 of my Irish and Scottish extended family. There is never a single scrap left.

Grate the red cabbage separately from the other ingredients, as it will turn everything red. And, if you're not serving straight away, layer the components. This could be on a platter, if serving at a party, or in a lunch box. Place the dressing on the bottom, noodles tossed with veg in the middle layer, then avocado, herbs and nuts sitting on the top. Then toss when you're ready to serve – if this is in a lunch box, just give it a good shake with the lid on. Tossing everything together at the very last moment will ensure everything stays fresh and zingy.

1   Preheat the oven to 180°C/160°C fan/350°F/gas mark 4 (if you don't have an air fryer).

2   Combine the lime juice, light soy sauce, maple syrup, toasted sesame oil and salt in a jug (pitcher) and mix well, to make the dressing. Check for seasoning and adjust if necessary. Set aside.

3   Toss the long-stemmed broccoli in the neutral oil and roast in the air fryer for 8 minutes at 200°C/400°F (cover the frilly bits with foil for the first 5 minutes, so that just the stems are poking out), or in the preheated oven for 15 minutes. Once charred, chop into 2.5cm (1in) pieces and add to a large mixing bowl. Add the carrot, cabbage, spring onions (scallions), coriander (cilantro) and mint.

4   Cook the noodles according to the packet instructions. Strain and rinse under cool water, separating the noodles with your fingers, to prevent them from sticking. Add the noodles to the mixing bowl, along with the dressing. Toss well using your hands.

5   Serve on a platter, individual plates or in lunch boxes, topped with the avocado, furikake and pistachios.

Minimal Effort Noodles

30+ MINUTES

Sichuan-style Green Bean Noodles

SERVES 2

1 tsp Sichuan peppercorns
2 nests medium egg noodles
1 tsp toasted sesame oil
2 tbsp light soy sauce
1 tsp dark soy sauce
1 tbsp oyster sauce
1 tsp light (soft) brown sugar
¼ tsp sea salt
1 tbsp neutral oil, plus extra
   to coat the pan
225g (8oz) green beans,
   tops trimmed
2 large garlic cloves, crushed
   or grated
1 small red chilli, finely diced
2.5cm (1in) ginger, peeled
   and grated
100g (3½oz) fatty pork mince
   (ground pork)
2 tbsp Shaoxing rice wine
2 dried red Chinese chillies
2 tbsp ya cai

Sichuanese dry-fried green beans (Gan Bian Si Ji Dou) is a traditional dish made up of blistered and charred green beans, with pork mince, aromatics, preserved mustard greens (ya cai) and a heady, spicy sauce, with Sichuan peppercorns. It is delicious on its own or served with rice. I love it combined with noodles, similar to Dou Jiao Men Mian, which is a Northern Chinese dish of pork and green beans, with noodles braised alongside in the sauce.

The green beans are typically shallow-fried until blistered but, in the spirit of efficiency and minimal washing up, I found that cooking them in a wok wiped with a very thin layer of oil, over a very high heat, blistered them quite well. Alternatively, dry-fry them in batches in the largest non-stick, heavy-based frying pan (skillet) you have, ensuring that there is ample space between each bean to allow the heat to circulate between them.

1   In a dry pan, add the Sichuan peppercorns and toast for 1 minute, stirring frequently, until fragrant. Grind these with a pestle and mortar or spice grinder, then sieve (strain) to remove the yellow husks. Set aside.

2   Cook the noodles according to the packet instructions. Drain and rinse under cool water, separating the noodles with your fingers, to prevent them from sticking. Toss with the sesame oil and set aside.

3   Combine the light soy, dark soy, oyster sauce, brown sugar and salt in a jug (pitcher) to make the sauce. Set aside.

4   Apply a small amount of neutral oil to a piece of paper towel and brush over a large non-stick, heavy-based frying pan (skillet) or wok, to create a thin coating. Set over a high heat. Once the pan is hot, add half the green beans. Leave these, without tossing or stirring, to blister for 3–4 minutes. Toss, then leave them again, until all sides are blistered and the beans look wrinkled and withered. Transfer them to a plate and set the pan back on the heat. Repeat with the remaining beans.

5   Add the 1 tbsp neutral oil, the garlic, chilli and ginger. Stir fry for 30 seconds, until fragrant. Add the pork, stir to combine and then leave for 1 minute, to allow the pork to gain some colour, before tossing and stir frying. Add the Shaoxing rice wine, dried chillies, ground Sichuan peppercorns, the green beans and ya cai. Stir fry for 2 minutes. Add the noodles, followed by the sauce and toss to combine. Serve immediately.

Salmon Mazesoba

SERVES 2

1 tbsp light soy sauce

1 tbsp toasted sesame oil

1 tsp mirin

1 tsp kecap manis

1 tbsp toasted sesame seeds

2 boneless salmon fillets

3 tbsp soy bean sauce

1 small courgette (zucchini),
thinly sliced

1 tsp neutral oil

1 tsp garlic salt

1 egg (or 2, depending on hunger)

2 nests somen or thin
wheat noodles

1 toasted nori sheet, cut into 4

1 spring onion (scallion),
finely sliced

1 tbsp crispy garlic

100g (3½oz) canned bamboo
shoots, strained and finely sliced

1 tbsp furikake

Mazesoba translates from Japanese to English as 'mixed up noodles' and it's one of my favourite ways to use up leftovers. Mazesoba began life as Taiwan Mazesoba, a dish made famous by Californian ramen chain Menya Hanabi in 2008. In this dish, several elements are arranged on top of a carb – in this case, it's noodles – and then mixed up and served with an egg on top.

1   Preheat the oven to 180°C/160°C fan/350°F/gas mark 4 (if you don't have an air fryer).

2   Combine the light soy sauce, sesame oil, mirin, kecap manis and sesame seeds in a jug (pitcher) to make the sauce. Mix well and set aside.

3   Brush the salmon with the soy bean sauce. Coat the courgette (zucchini) in the neutral oil. Cook both together in the air fryer for 12 minutes at 200°C/400°F, turning the courgette halfway through. Or, spread onto a baking tray and roast in the oven for 20 minutes until the salmon is just cooked through, charred on the outside and flaking easily, and the courgette are golden. Season the courgette with the garlic salt.

4   Meanwhile, bring a pot of water to the boil and drop in the egg. Set a timer for 6 minutes 45 seconds. After 2 minutes, drop in the noodles (or for the time suggested on the packet). When the timer sounds, pop the noodles and egg into a colander and strain. Pluck out the egg and allow to cool slightly before peeling and halving.

5   Flake the salmon from its skin and set aside. If you like the skin, put the skin back into the air fryer or oven to crisp up for 3–5 minutes. Place the nori squares in the air fryer for 30 seconds.

6   Divide the noodles between two bowls. Add half the sauce to each bowl and toss through the noodles. Arrange the spring onions (scallions), crispy garlic and courgette on top of the noodles. Add the flaked salmon and half an egg to each bowl. Crumble the nori and crunch up the salmon skin (if using) and serve on top, with the sliced bamboo shoots.

7   Garnish with furikake and serve immediately, while the noodles are still hot.

Beef and Charred Spring Onion Noodles

SERVES 2

For the marinade

1 tbsp neutral oil
2 tbsp fish sauce
1 tbsp light soy sauce
1 tbsp golden caster (superfine)
  sugar
2 garlic cloves, crushed or grated
1 tbsp cornflour (cornstarch)
1 large sirloin or ribeye steak

For the dressing

1 tbsp fish sauce
1 tbsp golden caster (superfine)
  sugar
1 tbsp lime juice
1 red bird's eye chilli, finely sliced
1 garlic clove, crushed or grated

For the noodles

2 nests pho noodles or wide
  rice noodles
1 small carrot, peeled
¼ cucumber, deseeded and
  sliced diagonally
1 small handful of coriander
  (cilantro), roughly chopped
2 tbsp roasted salted peanuts,
  crushed or chopped

For the spring onions (scallions)

1 tbsp neutral oil
6 spring onions (scallions), cleaned
  but left whole
1 tsp sea salt

This recipe utilizes a technique known as velveting, where a protein, usually beef or chicken, is marinated in cornflour (cornstarch) or sometimes bicarbonate of soda (baking soda) to make the meat soft and delicious when stir frying. It's a technique commonly used in Chinese cookery and in Chinese restaurants. If you've ever wondered how chefs create that deliciously browned but tender meat in stir fries or noodle dishes – this is how! Typically, you would marinate the meat for a little longer than stated here, but marinating for a shorter time still works a treat. The combination of the charred spring onion (scallion) and tender-but-crispy beef is simply dreamy.

1   To make the marinade, combine the neutral oil, fish sauce, light soy sauce, sugar, garlic and cornflour (cornstarch) in a shallow bowl. Add the steak and turn it a few times so it is completely covered. Set aside while you prepare the rest of the ingredients.

2   To make the dressing, combine the fish sauce, sugar, 3 tbsp water and the lime juice with the red bird's eye chilli and garlic. Mix well and set aside.

3   Cook or soak the rice noodles according to the packet instructions. Strain and rinse under cool water, separating the noodles with your fingers, to prevent them from sticking. Set aside.

4   Using a vegetable peeler, cut the carrot into very thin ribbons. Set aside.

5   Drizzle the neutral oil over the spring onions (scallions). Set a griddle pan, plancha or non-stick, heavy-based frying pan (skillet) over the highest heat you can. Once hot, add the spring onions (scallions) and allow them to grill on all sides until slightly charred and smoky. It can help to lay something flat and heavy on top of them, like a smaller pan. Once cooked, season with the salt and cut into 2.5cm (1in) pieces, then set aside.

6   In the same hot pan, cook the marinated steak for 3–4 minutes on either side (or to your liking) until crispy and brown. Allow to rest for 3–4 minutes while you assemble the bowls.

7   Divide the noodles between two bowls. Arrange the carrot and cucumber to one side, along with the coriander (cilantro), peanuts and charred spring onions (scallions). Add the dressing to two small dipping bowls.

8   Slice the steak against the grain and serve on top of the noodles.

Cashew Chicken Satay and Broccoli Noodles

SERVES 4

2 tbsp neutral oil

3 garlic cloves

5 dried red chillies, soaked in boiling water for 15 minutes, then chopped

100g (3½oz) dry roasted peanuts (unsalted) or 100g (3½oz) peanut butter

150g (5½oz) unsalted cashews or 150g (5½oz) cashew butter

400ml (14fl oz) coconut milk

1 tsp sea salt

2 tbsp golden caster (superfine) sugar

1 tbsp mild curry powder

2 tbsp kecap manis

4 skin-on, bone-in chicken thighs

200g (7oz) long-stemmed broccoli

1 tbsp olive oil

4 nests fresh egg noodles

4 tbsp Sichuan chilli oil or Lao Gan Ma Crispy Chilli Oil

3 spring onions (scallions), finely sliced

The word satay (or sate) refers to skewered and grilled meat; however, the name is often mistakenly confused with the sauce that satay is frequently served with. Satay sauce is usually a creamy, smooth, nutty sauce made with peanuts and light soy sauce. While it originated in Indonesia, it can now be found in many other Southeast Asian cuisines. Once upon a time, I would serve skewered chicken with noodles and a peanut sauce, until one weeknight I shoved the chicken thighs under the grill whole. And in the spirit of efficiency, this recipe remained that way.

1   Preheat the oven to 180°C/160°C fan/350°F/gas mark 4.

2   Heat the oil in a non-stick, heavy-based frying pan (skillet) over a medium heat and add the whole garlic cloves and chopped chillies. Fry for 30 seconds to 1 minute or until fragrant. Pour the aromatics and oil into a high-speed blender along with the nuts, coconut milk, salt, sugar, curry powder and kecap manis. Whizz into a smooth sauce.

3   Add the chicken thighs to a baking tray and cover in the sauce. Bake in the oven for 30 minutes.

4   Once the chicken has been in the oven for 10 minutes, coat the broccoli in the olive oil and arrange on a separate baking tray. Place in the oven on the shelf below the chicken and roast for 20 minutes.

5   5 minutes before the chicken and broccoli are ready, cook the egg noodles according to the packet instructions. Drain and rinse with cold water to prevent clumping. Serve the noodles topped with a chicken thigh, a portion of broccoli and plenty of satay sauce. Drizzle with the chilli oil and garnish with the spring onions (scallions).

Beef Japchae

SERVES 4

For the beef

1 tbsp light soy sauce

1 tbsp mirin

1 garlic clove, grated or crushed

¼ tsp sea salt

1 tsp cornflour (cornstarch)

1 ribeye or sirloin steak, cut into
thin strips

1 tbsp neutral oil

For the sauce

4 dried shiitake mushrooms

4 tbsp light soy sauce

2 tsp dark soy sauce

4 tbsp maple syrup

¼ tsp freshly ground black pepper

1 tbsp toasted sesame seeds

1 tbsp toasted sesame oil

For the omelette

neutral oil, to coat the pan

1 spring onion (scallion),
finely sliced

3 eggs, beaten

For the vegetables

½ onion, sliced

1 red (bell) pepper, finely shredded

1 small carrot, peeled and
finely shredded

2 heads pak choi (bok choy), stems
removed and leaves separated

For the noodles

280g (10oz) dangmyeon noodles

Japchae is a Korean dish of meat and vegetables, with Korean glass noodles, dangmyeon, which are made from sweet potato starch. They have a bouncy texture and a subtly sweet flavour – very different from rice vermicelli. Japchae translates as 'mixed vegetables', as this dish was once served without noodles; however, over time, the dangmyeon became the main feature, probably because of their standout texture. There are many variations of Japchae, such as bean sprout (Kongnamul Japchae) or mixed seafood (Haemul-Japchae).

For this dish, each element is prepared separately, then combined just before serving. It's great hot or at room temperature and can be enjoyed as a main meal, side dish or lunch box. The meat and vegetables work well with rice, instead of the noodles, too.

1   In a bowl, combine the light soy sauce, mirin, garlic, salt and cornflour (cornstarch), add the beef slices and allow to marinate while you prepare the rest of the ingredients.

2   Bring a pot of water to the boil – this is to cook the noodles at the final step. Meanwhile, soak the shiitake mushrooms for the sauce in a mug of boiling water. Combine the light soy, dark soy, maple syrup, black pepper, sesame seeds and sesame oil in a jug (pitcher) and set aside.

3   Brush a non-stick, heavy-based frying pan (skillet) with a light coating of neutral oil and place over a medium heat. In a small bowl, add the sliced spring onion (scallion), eggs and a pinch of salt and beat together. Add the egg mixture to the frying pan (skillet) and twirl the pan to make a thin omelette. Cook for 1–2 minutes, flip it over with a fish slice and cook for another 1–2 minutes or until cooked through. Then, transfer to a chopping board and, when cool enough to handle, roll into a long tube and slice into ½cm (¼in) rounds. Set aside.

4   Brush the same pan with a little more oil, if needed, and add the onion. Stir fry over a high heat for 2–3 minutes or until slightly softened and charred on the edges. Transfer to the chopping board, next to the omelette slices, and set aside.

5   Next, again with a little more oil if needed, fry the red (bell) pepper for 2–3 minutes or until just softened and the edges begin to char. Transfer to the chopping board, next to the onions, and set aside.

6   Add the carrots, and again more oil if needed, and fry for 3–4 minutes or until just softened, but keeping their shape. Transfer to the chopping board and set aside.

7   Remove the shiitake mushrooms from their soaking liquor, cut off and discard the stems and slice thinly.

8   Heat the 1 tbsp of oil in the same pan over a medium-high heat. Scoop the steak out of the marinade, allowing any excess to drip off before adding it to the pan. Let it sit in the hot oil for a minute or so, to crisp up, before stir frying. Once the beef is browned and crispy all over, remove from the pan and place on the chopping board next to the rest of the prepared ingredients.

9   Add the pak choi (bok choy) leaves to the pan of boiling water and blanch for 1 minute, until just wilted but still vibrant green. Remove from the pan and set aside. Add the noodles to the water and cook according to the packet instructions. Tip the noodles into a colander and immediately transfer to a large mixing bowl (or a large saucepan if you don't have a mixing bowl big enough).

10   Add all of the prepared vegetables, omelette slices and meat to the noodles and toss – this is best done with the hands (wear gloves if you prefer) or tongs – combining everything well. Add the sauce and toss to coat. Serve immediately.

Roast Chicken Ramen

SERVES 4

1 medium roast-in-the-bag
  chicken
1L (35fl oz) chicken bone broth
5cm (2in) ginger, peeled: 1 tbsp
  grated and the rest sliced into 3
4 spring onions (scallions), whites
  and greens separated, greens
  finely sliced, whites left whole
2 eggs
4 tbsp light soy sauce
4 tbsp mirin
1 handful of dried, shredded black
  fungus mushrooms or 4 dried
  shiitake mushrooms
4 nests ramen noodles
2 large garlic cloves, grated
3 tbsp neutral oil
2 tsp chicken bouillon powder
2 tsp light (soft) brown sugar
2 tbsp toasted sesame oil
1 toasted nori sheet, cut into 4

Using a good-quality, fresh chicken stock will make a huge difference here. I wouldn't usually suggest roasting a whole chicken in a cookbook aimed at speed and efficiency, but the roast-in-the-bag whole chickens you can get are so easy and pretty foolproof. You can shove them in the oven, set a timer, and walk away. The foil tray also collects a huge amount of juice and fat that can be added to the stock for a quick injection of body, creating a luscious broth without simmering bones for hours. Almost every cuisine has its own variation of chicken noodle soup and this one is similar to a Japanese Tori Chintan Shoyu Ramen – clear chicken broth (tori chintan) seasoned with soy (shoyu) with ramen noodles.

1   Roast the chicken according to the packet instructions. Set a timer.

2   While the chicken is cooking, bring the bone broth to a gentle barely-there simmer in a large saucepan. Add the sliced ginger and the spring onion (scallion) whites and let the broth sit, over the lowest heat, while the chicken roasts. You can do this in a slow cooker, if you'd rather.

3   In another pan, boil the eggs for 6 minutes 45 seconds. Rinse under cold water to cool them and then peel.

4   Combine the light soy sauce and mirin in a small bowl or mug and place the eggs in the marinade. Place the black fungus or shiitake mushrooms in another mug of boiling water to soak.

5   When the chicken is cooked, remove from the oven and leave to cool for 10–20 minutes before opening the bag. Be careful not to upturn the tray containing all the juices. Once the bag is open, lift out the chicken and set onto a plate. Pour the chicken juices into the chicken broth.

6   Cook the noodles according to the packet instructions. Drain and rinse under cool water, separating the noodles with your fingers, to prevent them from sticking. Set aside.

7   Shred the chicken meat from the carcass and set aside. I like including the skin, but you don't have to.

8 Divide the grated garlic and ginger between 4 large, deep bowls. Heat the neutral oil until smoking. Carefully, pour the oil over the ginger and garlic in each bowl – it will cause a little spluttering.

9 Remove the black fungus or shiitake mushrooms from their soaking liquor. If using shiitake, remove the stems and slice thinly. Set aside.

10 Pluck the eggs out of their marinade and halve them. Divide the egg marinade between the bowls and stir into the ginger and garlic oil. In each bowl, add ½ tsp chicken bouillon powder, ½ tsp light (soft) brown sugar and ½ tbsp toasted sesame oil.

11 Pluck the ginger slices and spring onion whites from the steaming broth and discard. Divide the broth between the four bowls, mixing well to combine and dissolve the sugar and bouillon powder.

12 Sit the noodles in the broth and top with the mushrooms, shredded chicken, spring onion greens, nori and a marinated egg half.

Miso Roast Tomato and Pork Belly Soba

SERVES 2

2 tbsp white miso
3 tbsp light soy sauce
2 tsp toasted sesame oil
250g (9oz) baby plum tomatoes (mixed colours are nice, but not essential), stems removed
4 large garlic cloves, peeled
1 tsp sea salt
1 tsp maple syrup
¼ tsp ground black pepper
1 tbsp Chinkiang black rice vinegar
1 tbsp neutral oil
120g (4¼oz) pork belly slice, finely sliced
2 eggs
2 nests dried soba noodles
1 tbsp furikake

During the summertime, when there is a glut of tomatoes, my favourite thing to do is to slow roast them in batches, with plenty of whole garlic and white miso. I then make sauce or soup, serve them simply on toast or, as here, with noodles.

Slow roasted tomatoes obviously take some time, which is against the grain of this book completely, so I would suggest using baby tomatoes to speed up the process a little. If you have an air fryer, even better.

1   Preheat the oven to 180°C/160°C fan/350°F/gas mark 4.

2   Combine the miso, 1 tbsp of the light soy sauce and the sesame oil in a jug (pitcher) until the mixture is slightly runny. In a baking tray, toss the tomatoes and whole garlic cloves in the miso/soy/sesame oil, allowing plenty of room between them. Sprinkle with the salt and roast in the oven for 30–45 minutes, or until the tomatoes are withered and darkened (but not brown or burned). If using an air fryer, dress the tomatoes and garlic cloves and tip them into the roasting pan of the air fryer. Set to 200°C/400°F and roast for 10 minutes on the 'air fry' setting.

3   Meanwhile, combine the remaining 2 tbsp light soy sauce, the maple syrup, black pepper and black rice vinegar in a jug to make the dressing. Set aside.

4   Heat the neutral oil in a non-stick, heavy-based frying pan (skillet) over a medium-high heat. Fry the pork belly slices for 2–3 minutes on either side, until crispy and golden.

5   Bring a pan of water to the boil. Drop in the eggs and set a timer for 6 minutes 45 seconds. After 2 minutes, add the soba noodles (or time according to the packet instructions). Once the timer sounds, strain the noodles and eggs. Pluck the eggs out of the strainer and allow to cool slightly before peeling.

6   When the tomatoes are ready, pluck out the garlic cloves and roughly chop them. Stir them through the dressing.

7   Divide the noodles into two bowls and add the tomatoes on top, along with the dressing. Stir everything together, pressing the tomatoes slightly to squeeze out their juices. Top with the crispy pork belly slices and a soft boiled egg, halved. Garnish with a sprinkling of furikake.

Rice Noodles with Spring Rolls

SERVES 2

For the pickle

5 tbsp white rice vinegar

2 tbsp golden caster (superfine) sugar

1 tbsp sea salt

1 small carrot, grated

For the noodles

2 nests dried rice vermicelli noodles

1 gem lettuce, finely sliced

¼ cucumber, deseeded and sliced on the diagonal

1 small handful of mint, roughly chopped

1 small handful of coriander (cilantro), roughly chopped

6 Vietnamese egg rolls or spring rolls (frozen or from the takeaway)

For the dressing

2 tbsp golden caster (superfine) sugar

2 tbsp lime juice

3 tbsp Vietnamese fish sauce

2 large garlic cloves, grated

1 red bird's eye chilli, finely chopped

'Bun', in Vietnamese, means rice vermicelli. I've seen bun referred to as a noodle salad before, as the noodles are served at room temperature, alongside cucumber, pickled carrot and daikon, shredded lettuce, and fresh herbs with a dressing. When served with beef, the dish is called Bun Bo Xao; and when served with Vietnamese egg rolls, it's Bun Cha Gio, which is my favourite way to eat rice noodles.

However, egg rolls, or spring rolls, are not my favourite thing to prepare. It's fun, yes, but also time consuming. So, in this recipe, like in many others in this book, I utilize takeaway add-ons. That is, when I am in Chinatown stopping in at my favourite Vietnamese place for Banh Mi, I always buy egg rolls for another time. I'll keep them in the fridge to reheat when I'm ready to make Bun. Reheating spring rolls is quickest in an air fryer, but you can also re-fry them, or reheat in the oven. You can also buy very good-quality spring rolls and egg rolls by the bag in the freezer section of East and Southeast Asian supermarkets.

Typically, Bun would be served with pickled daikon and carrot. I suggest a quick pickle here with carrot alone. This is because it can be difficult to find a small daikon, and I don't have many recipes in this book for the rest of the vegetable, so I've left it out to reduce waste. If you want to add daikon to your pickle, though, do go ahead! You can, of course, pickle the whole thing and make a big batch – these pickles are great on Banh Mi and Bun – just use an equal weight in carrot.

1   Preheat the oven to 180°C/160°C fan/350°F/gas mark 4 (if you don't have an air fryer).

2   To make the pickle, combine the rice vinegar, sugar, salt and 3 tbsp water in a small bowl and stir until everything has dissolved. Add the carrot and leave for 5 minutes while you prepare everything else.

3   Cook or soak the vermicelli noodles according to the packet instructions. Drain and rinse under cool water to keep them springy. Divide between two bowls.

4   To make the dressing, combine the sugar, lime juice, fish sauce, garlic and bird's eye chilli with 100ml (3½oz) hot water in a jug (pitcher). Decant into two dipping bowls and serve alongside the noodles.

5   Arrange the lettuce, cucumber and herbs on top of the noodles.

6   Cook the Vietnamese egg or spring rolls according to the packet instructions, if using frozen. If using takeaway spring rolls, reheat these in the air fryer at 200°C/400°F for 6 minutes or in the preheated oven for 15 minutes, or until crispy. Once cooked, cut each into 3 segments and arrange on top of the noodles.

7   Scoop out the carrot from its pickle juice and allow any excess to drip off, before arranging on top of the noodles. Serve while the spring/egg rolls are still hot.

Suppliers

The below stock a wide range of East and Southeast Asian ingredients, including store-cupboard, fresh and frozen ingredients, and cookware.

TUK TUK MART

tuktukmart.co.uk

Filipino, Malaysian and Indonesian ingredients

ORIENTAL MART

orientalmart.co.uk

Fresh, frozen and store-cupboard ingredients

STARRY MART

starrymart.co.uk

A wide range of Japanese and Korean ingredients

SOUS CHEF

souschef.co.uk

A wide range of ingredients

WING YIP

wingyip.com

A wide range of store-cupboard ingredients

H MART

hmart.co.uk | hmart.com

Fresh, frozen and store-cupboard Korean ingredients

SUSHI SUSHI

sushisushi.co.uk

A wide range of Japanese ingredients

JAPAN CENTRE

japancentre.com

A wide range of Japanese ingredients

MALA MARKER

themalamarket.com

For premium Sichuanese ingredients

EFOODDEPOT

efooddepot.com

A wide range of Japanese and Thai ingredients

YAMIBUY

yamibuy.com

Great for Japanese, Korean and Chinese ingredients

BOROUGH BROTH CO

boroughbroth.co.uk

I love the Borough Broth Co's bone broths for quick and easy broths with good body. You can keep them in the freezer until you need them.

KOYA

koya.co.uk

For mail-order fresh udon and readymade dashi.

Further Reading

Here's a non-exhaustive selection of resources that I love and cook from myself regularly, from chefs and cooks that I respect immensely.

Websites

KOREANBAPSANG.COM

You can find great versions of Beef Japchae recipes by food writer Ro Hyo-sun here.

REDHOUSESPICE.COM

I love Wei Guo's recipe for egg and tomato stir fry.

SHESIMMERS.COM

Leela Punyaratabandhu published a five-part series on Pad Thai, covering everything you could wish to know about it – and I would highly recommend checking it out if you want to learn about the intricacies of this famous noodle dish.

MAANGCHI.COM

Maangchi, aka Emily Kim, is a Korean YouTuber and recipe developer. I love her recipes – they are foolproof – and her cookery videos are so much fun.

JUSTONECOOKBOOK.COM

Delicious and modern Japanese recipes from home cook Nami.

THEWOKSOFLIFE.COM

Family-run, Chinese recipe blog that was recently published into its own cookbook! One of my all-time favourite blogs, with a wealth of recipes, guides and tutorials.

OMNIVORESCOOKBOOK.COM

Modern Chinese recipe blog from writer, recipe developer and photographer Maggie Zhu.

Cookbooks

Aye, MiMi, *Mandalay* (Bloomsbury Absolute, 2019)

Chung, Amy and Emily, *The Rangoon Sisters* (Ebury Press, 2020)

Diem Pham, Thuy, *The Little Viet Kitchen* (Absolute Press, 2018)

Han Lee, Shu, *Chicken and Rice* (Fig Tree, 2016)

Huang, Ching-He, *Wok On* (Kyle Books, 2019)

Kaul, Rosheen and Hu, Joanna, *Chinese-ish* (Murdoch Books, 2022)

Lee, Lara, *Coconut & Sambal* (Bloomsbury Publishing, 2020)

Lee, Mandy, *The Art of Escapism Cooking* (William Morrow, 2019)

Leung, Bill and Kaitlin, *The Woks of Life* (Random House Inc, 2022)

Liu, Betty, *My Shanghai* (Harper Design, 2021)

Luu, Uyen, *Vietnamese* (Hardie Grant, 2021)

Scott, Su, *Rice Table* (Quadrille, 2023)

Wee, Sharon, *Growing Up in a Nonya Kitchen* (Marshall Cavendish International Ltd, 2021)

West, Da-Hae and Gareth, *K Food* (Mitchell Beazley, 2016)

Yenbamroong, Kris, *Night + Market* (Clarkson Potter, 2017)

Yin, Mandy, *Sambal Shiok* (Quadrille, 2021)

Young, Grace and Richardson, Alan, *The Breath of a Wok* (Simon and Schuster, 2004)

Zhu, Maggie, *Chinese Homestyle* (Rock Point, 2022)

Index

Thanks

It takes a lot of people to pull a cookbook together, and the very first step in that process is somebody believing your work is worth publishing. So, I'd like to thank my editor, Stacey, for constantly believing in me and trusting my ideas. Thank you to Hannah and Emily for your creative genius and for bringing such character to my books. Thank you to India and Magnus for capturing my food so beautifully and for bringing so much light and laughter to the set. Thank you Tamara, Emma and Charlotte for making my recipes look so appealing and delicious. Thank you Ruth and the team for everything you do behind the scenes to help share the book with the world.

I wrote and shot this book whilst going through the mill with an active autoimmune disease, and it simply wouldn't have been possible without the support of a lot of people. At home, Sloth, doing more than the lion's share of housework and childcare, to enable me to rest and to write and to edit. The whole team on the photoshoot, where I spent a large percentage of the days horizontal on the sofa on set. And every single person involved in the publishing process, for your patience and for taking the pressure off when I needed more time. Thank you all.

Publishing Director Sarah Lavelle

Commissioning Editor Stacey Cleworth

Art Direction and Design Emily Lapworth

Cover and Illustrations Han Valentine

Photographers India Hobson & Magnus Edmondson

Food Stylist Tamara Vos

Food Stylist Assistants Emma Cantlay
& Charlotte Whatcott

Prop Stylist Max Robinson

Head of Production Stephen Lang

Senior Production Controller Katie Jarvis

First published in 2023 by Quadrille,
an imprint of Hardie Grant Publishing

Quadrille
52–54 Southwark Street
London SE1 1UN
quadrille.com

Text © Pippa Middlehurst 2023
Photography © India Hobson & Magnus Edmondson 2023
Design and layout © Quadrille 2023

Cataloguing in Publication Data: a catalogue record
for this book is available from the British Library.

9781787139541

Printed in China